how to BE a GREAT employee

by Thomas Smith

Top Dog
Press

how to
BE a GREAT employee

GreatEmployee.net

Creative Employment Access Centre
103-555   4th Street
Courtenay, B.C.   V9N 1H3
(250)-334-3119

Top Dog
Press

Copyright © 2013 Thomas Smith

ISBN: 1489583009
ISBN-13: 978-1489583000

INDEX

Copyright 2002 by Randy Glasbergen.
www.glasbergen.com

GLASBERGEN

"I didn't get Employee of the Month or
Employee of the Week, but I was fourth
runner up for Employee of the Nanosecond."

"When I hear someone say that life is hard,
I am always tempted to ask, compared to
what?" —Stephen J. Harris

Why Read This Book?

Or, why improve at all? Maybe you're happy with your life exactly as it is. Maybe there is no need for improvement of any kind. Maybe you don't need any help or advice because you already have everything figured out for yourself. Or, maybe you could use a little assistance with improving your job, your career, as well as your life. . .

And you're up to the challenge.

"I don't have any references, but 4 out of 5 phone psychics say I'm destined for greatness."

So the reason to read this book is that no matter how great your life already is or isn't, this book brings an opportunity for you to grow further. This book on how to be a great success is a collection of ideas and techniques on how to make all parts of your life happier, calmer, more successful, and better.

"I'm looking for a mentor who can show me how to get rich without boring me with a lot of advice."

> ## "Things do not change, we change."
> ## —Henry David Thoreau, 100's of years ago

It's true. We cannot expect the world to change to meet our wants and needs. We cannot rely on the other people in our lives to do the changing. We need to do the changing. This is how we grow and make our lives better...by changing.

Speaking of the World

Many of us have the tendency to believe one of two things about our role in the world: the world revolves around us and our needs, or that the world's out to get us.

Let's clear up both myths, beginning with the world revolving around you, or me, for that matter. The world does not revolve around us. Scientists have proven it. Here's the proof. The world has been around for five billion years. You and me—I don't know your age, but we've certainly been around for less than 100 years. That's a fraction of the time that the world has been here. Therefore, how can the world revolve around you or me? Or here's another question: If the world revolved around us, then what was the world revolving around before there was a you or a me?

Now let's do an exercise to clear up myth number 2, that somehow the world is always out to get you. It might interest you to know that there are exactly 193 countries in the world according to the United Nations. Your exercise is to circle the names of any countries that you have never heard of.

Afghanistan	Chad	Ghana	Liberia	Norway	Sri Lanka
Albania	Chile	Greece	Libya	Oman	Sudan
Algeria	China	Grenada	Liechtenstein	Pakistan	Suriname
Andorra	Columbia	Guatemala	Lithuania	Palau	Swaziland
Angola	Comoros	Guinea	Luxembourg	Panama	Sweden
Antigua	Congo	Guinea-Bissau	Macedonia	Papua New Guinea	Switzerland
Argentina	Congo, Republic	Guyana	Madagascar	Paraguay	Syria
Armenia	Costa Rica	Haiti	Malawi	Peru	Tajikistan
Australia	Cote d'Ivoire	Honduras	Malaysia	Philippines	Tanzania
Austria	Croatia	Hungary	Maldives	Poland	Thailand
Azerbaijan	Cuba	Iceland	Mali	Portugal	Togo
Bahamas	Cyprus	India	Malta	Qatar	Tonga
Bahrain	Czech Republic	Indonesia	Marshall Islands	Romania	Trinidad Tobago
Bangladesh	Denmark	Iran	Mauritania	Russia	Tunisia
Barbados	Djibouti	Iraq	Mauritius	Rwanda	Turkey
Belarus	Dominica	Ireland	Mexico	Saint Kitts	Turkmenistan
Belgium	Dominion Republic	Israel	Micronesia	Saint Vincent	Tuvalu
Belize	East Timor	Italy	Moldova	Samoa	Uganda
Benin	Ecuador	Jamaica	Monaco	San Marino	Ukraine
Bhutan	Egypt	Japan	Mongolia	Sao Tome	United Arab Emirates
Bolivia	El Salvador	Jordan	Montenegro	Saudi Arabia	United Kingdom
Bosnia	Equator Guinea	Kazakhstan	Morocco	Senegal	United States
Botswana	Eritrea	Kenya	Mozambique	Serbia	Uruguay
Brazil	Estonia	Kiribati	Myanmar	Seychelles	Uzbekistan
Brunei	Ethiopia	Korea, North	Namibia	Sierra Leone	Vanuatu
Bulgaria	Fiji	Korea, South	Nauru	Singapore	Vatican City
Burkina Faso	Finland	Kuwait	Nepal	Slovakia	Venezuela
Cambodia	France	Kyrgyzstan	Netherlands	Slovenia	Vietnam
Cameroon	Gabon	Laos	New Zealand	Solomon Islands	Yemen
Canada	Gambia	Latvia	Nicaragua	Somalia	Zambia
Cape Verde	Georgia	Lebanon	Niger	South Africa	Zimbabwe
Central African	Germany	Lesotho	Nigeria	Spain	

If you're like most people, I bet you have quite a few circles around countries you've never heard of. Which proves that there are lots of countries that you've never even heard of. If you haven't heard of them, chances are they haven't heard of you, either. So, how can the entire world be out to get you?

Do You Like Your Job?

People fall into a few categories when it comes to their job. They either love what they do and couldn't possibly picture doing anything else. Or the opposite extreme, they don't enjoy their job at all. Most people tend to fall somewhere in-between these extremes, neither loving nor hating their job. But, even the worst job can always be worse. . . My worst job ever was when I was in London, England and I desperately needed money. I took a job as a door-to-door fire extinguisher salesman. My supervisor gave me some lighter fluid, matches and the fire extinguisher I was supposed to try to sell. I was then dropped off in a strange neighborhood to start selling. The idea was for me to ring the doorbell, light a fire on the person's porch before they even had a chance to ask what I was doing, and then put out the fire using the fire extinguisher. I made a very interesting discovery. Most people don't like having someone ring their doorbell and then set fire to their porch. That was my worst job. The worst job I've ever heard of anyone else having was someone who was actually hired to be a quality taster in a cat food factory. So what's the worst job you've ever had?

"You want to feed the elephants, fat chance...You have to earn that promotion."

"Every job, no matter how small, is important. To reinforce this point, I'm awarding Employee Of The Month to my belt."

So What's This Book Going To Do For You?

There is a Buddhist legend about a woman who loses her ring while walking in a back alley one day. When she gets home she realizes that the ring is gone, so she goes back to search for it. By the time she begins searching it's nighttime—the alley is dark and scary. So, she decides to search for the ring in the street instead, where there are streetlights. The woman obviously can't find the ring in the street, even though it is light, because the ring is not there.

This is how our problems and challenges tend to work, too. We tend to look for our answers in the same familiar places, even when we haven't found successful answers in these places or ways before. Sometimes we need to risk entering less-er-known and even frightening places because that is where our true answers often lie...in the unknown.

And Here's One More Important Topic . . .

Here's an interesting tidbit. A major survey was done that asked people what their biggest problem was in life. Now you might have thought most people would answer things like not having enough money, family problems, health issues or relationship issues. These are all big problems for a lot of people. It wasn't one of these things though. The biggest problem, according to 75% of people asked—that's 3 out of every 4 of us—was a **lack of confidence.**

Lack of confidence is what causes people to live their lives well below their potential, never attempting many of the things that they are capable of doing, if only they would try. A lack of confidence is like a rainstorm drowning out happiness, success and friendships. When people act out, get angry and display disruptive behavior, a lack of confidence is often what's behind it.

So what's the solution? Books and books have been written on the subject, but I believe the cure for a lack of confidence comes down to one thing more than anything else: a positive attitude. From a positive attitude springs optimism, and from optimism comes confidence. A positive attitude leads to people liking you and wanting to be around you, which brings confidence, too.

Copyright 2003 by Randy Glasbergen.
www.glasbergen.com

"Welcome to my motivational seminar. If you are here tonight instead of home on your sofa, then you're already a motivated person and don't need me! Good night and thank you for coming."

Choices at Work... We Choose:

1. Whether we excel or just slide by doing the bare minimum.

2. To be self-centered and inconsiderate or respectful, kind and helpful.

3. When setbacks happen we can be crushed and feel sorry for ourselves, or we can look for strength and then keep trying.

4. We can learn only the bare minimum, or we can view learning as a great opportunity to benefit ourselves.

5. We can be closed minded to new ideas or be open minded.

6. We can have goals and desires, putting effort behind them, or we can stand still, never making progress.

Most important, we are free to choose our attitude. This is the most important choice we will make because it has everything to do with how well we succeed in our jobs and our life.

Why be a Great Employee? Why Not Slide By?

Okay, you do the math. Most people work around 40 hours a week. Counting the time it takes to get ready for work, drive or take the bus to work and then come home, it's probably more like 50 hours a week. There are 168 hours in a week, but we spend around 68 of them sleeping, getting ready to sleep, brushing our teeth and washing up for bed. So after we take away those 68 hours, there are 100 hours left each week—and half of those hours have to do with working. It only makes sense that something that occupies half of our time should be important and we should want to get the most out of it. Besides, if we make a point of enjoying and getting the most from the workday then we will probably keep that same attitude rolling along after we go home, getting the most from our time spent away from work, too. On the other hand, if we make work lousy, chances are the rest of our life will follow and be lousy, too.

Besides, doing your best feels good. Doing your best leads to appreciation and respect from coworkers, clients, customers, and supervisors and that feels good, too. It also leads to feeling pride in yourself and nothing feels better than a sense of self-worth. Most of us have no choice but to put in the hours, so we may as well do our best and get the most we can while we're working.

Copyright 2000 by Randy Glasbergen.   www.glasbergen.com

"I got paid 50 million dollars this week. Do you think it's a mistake or did my boss finally realize how valuable I am?"

How Does This Book Work?

This book is about how to succeed where you work, but it's also about how to improve the other parts of your life as well, including your family relationships, your friendships, meeting your dreams and expectations, and in all kinds of ways how you go about living your life.

It's like anything else: The more you put into reading this book then the more you'll get out of it.

Take as long as you like to read this book. One great way to read it is a chapter at a time, perhaps one chapter each day. There are no rules other than this one—you get back what you put in.

Here are some of the exercises and tools you will find scattered throughout this book designed to get you to think and examine your life. For instance:

You're throwing a dinner party and can invite any 3 guests, living or dead. They can be famous people, a hero, people from history who fascinate you, or a family member. Who would you invite?

Who would You Invite?

The Value of Quotes

Over the years, billions of people have said trillions of things and some of them have been brilliant. Throughout this book are quotes, which if you think about them, may impact your life. Some of them are on the funny side, teaching lessons with a humorous twist. Others are clever, and still others are just plain great advice. Imagine being able to sit down to lunch with Albert Einstein, or John F. Kennedy, or even Madonna. Wouldn't it be incredibly valuable to hear their words as learning tools? That's what quotes give us, the best advice from very smart people.

Techniques to Assist Change

This book will give you many useful techniques. For instance, the following is a technique dating back to Ancient Greece:

Understanding the 'Law of Attraction'

No, the Law of Attraction is not about the proper way to apply makeup. It's a law about the universe and how things work. The Law of Attraction states that when you expect the worst, then the worst will happen to you, but when you expect the best, then the best is more likely to happen to you. Whatever we think about the most is what actually tends to happen. So, if you want good things, then learn to expect good things to happen. If you want fewer things to worry about then stop worrying so much. If you want to be happy, then expect happiness to happen. That's how The Law of Attraction works.

Then Sam tried counting sheep, but the sheep came down with Mad Sheep Disease.

Life Tips

Life Tips are philosophies which you might find useful or inspiring. The example below is a repeat of a tip given earlier in this chapter.

This is Life's Ultimate Rule: **You get back what you put in.**

"I'm transferring you to another office, Dave. Many of us are on low-carb diets and you look like a french fry."

Exercises

Scattered throughout this book are a few exercises. None of the exercises will take you more than a few minutes to complete. Most of these exercises will be fun, and you'll find them extremely useful in understanding your own path to happiness and success. So here it is, the first exercise:

> Write down one thing about the way that you are which you would like to improve or change altogether. (Examples: too angry, too impatient, often disorganized, too bossy, too serious, overly shy)

Full Day Exercises

A full-day exercise is where you test a new behavior for a day and see how it feels, as well as how others respond to you. **Here's Your First One:**

> In the prior exercise you identified an area where you'd like to improve yourself or change completely. Spend an entire workday making that change as best as you can. For instance, if the improvement that you listed is to put in more effort and not be distracted, then for this one day, follow through. If you mess up, that's okay. Just keep trying.

"I'll take the positive and a side order of pleasant".

"People are just as happy as they make up their minds to be?"
—Abraham Lincoln

Attitude. . . it's not the biggest word in the English language. The biggest word is **pneumonoultramicroscopicsilicovolcanokoniosis**, with 45 letters.

Attitude has only 9 letters. Attitude, on the other hand, is the key to just about everything in life. It's the key to success at work, and the key to success outside of work, your health, relationships—it's the engine that drives just about everything. Our attitude is what makes our lives absolutely fantastic, fulfilled and content—or a bad attitude can make our lives a shadow of what life can be.

For years people have been searching for the secret of happiness. They've gone about this chase for happiness in a gazillion different ways. Some have joined communes to live with nature, or monasteries to meditate. Others have read bushels of books, attended buckets of seminars, and taken blue pills, green pills and red pills. They've changed their relationships, jobs, cities, homes, or cars, all in the constant search for happiness.

"If we do things only when we're in the mood...then what if we're never in the mood?"

Here's the truth. Happiness is not a search. It's not a place, or a thing, a possession or a person. It's certainly not a pill. A pill is just temporary happiness, with a whole lot of unhappiness to follow.

If you've treated happiness as a treasure hunt, believing that happiness is a new car or a big-screen television—whenever you find that treasure chest full of things you think you want, you'll probably be disappointed. It won't magically change your life, at least not permanently. It may not even be a treasure at all.

"A chest full of 40-Cent-Off coupons for deodorant at Food Planet... You call that a treasure?"

The Secret of Happiness Is . . .

People have been searching for the secret to happiness for at least 10,000 years. A positive attitude is a great part of the true secret. Who do you think is happier, your average Hollywood celebrity or someone who is content in their life, well liked by their friends, and does their best at work and most everywhere else?

A survey was done of lottery winners who won over a million dollars, a year after their lottery win. The majority of the big money winners actually were unhappier with their lives after they became rich. Here's what else is interesting. The big lottery winners who were the happiest were the ones who stayed in their same jobs and kept their same homes and friends. The only thing they changed was buying a few extra things. Money or things won't make you happy—**your attitude** makes you happy.

> "Money won't buy you happiness. . . but everyone wants to find out for themselves." —Zig Zigler

Bad Attitude Versus Good Attitude

With a **good attitude** you choose to be happy. Life isn't perfect, but you look for ways to be optimistic and hopeful. You find reasons to smile. People like being around you because we're all drawn to upbeat people with **good attitudes**. When you have a **bad attitude**, you actually look for ways and reasons to be miserable. You're cynical and pessimistic—life kind of sucks. Do people like being around you? No, not very much.

You know you have a Bad Attitude at Work when...

1. At your last 10 jobs you received a standing ovation... for quitting.

2. You ask for a stress leave day...your first day of work.

3. You wear a shirt to work that says, "I Have a Bad Attitude and I'm Proud of It."

© 2000 Randy Glasbergen.
www.glasbergen.com

GLASBERGEN

"Your bad attitude was starting to affect the others. That's much better."

The Amazing Race

On the television show The Amazing Race, people travel to different destinations, completing a task in each place, to win a million dollars? In this section we're going to travel all around the world in search of what a great attitude is. There's no million dollars, but the prize might be a Great Attitude!

That's not bad !!!

Attitude Destination 1: New York City---World Trade Center: **To Find: Putting Others First**

Here's my story about putting others first. It took place the day the Twin Towers came down. There were lots of people who put others first that day. One of them was the son of one of my closest friends. His name was Thomas Edward Jurgens, people called him Tommy. He was 26. Tommy had been a messed-up kid, but had gotten his life together, and was engaged to be married. Tommy worked as a bailiff in the court building a block away from the World Trade Center. When the first plane hit on September 11 there was a call for anyone who knew first aid to go to the site and help. Nobody was forced to go into such a dangerous situation. Tommy volunteered. Tommy's remains were never found. It's believed Tommy was in the food court, helping with first aid, when more than a 100 stories of building collapsed on top of him.

Putting others first means: kindness, consideration, compassion and realizing that other people have needs, not just you. Putting others first in your personal life means your family and friends. In your workplace it's your coworkers. It's also people you hardly know at all. Sometimes it's helping people you have never even met, like Tommy did. Occasionally it's an act of heroism. Most often it's just doing something nice for someone, without a reason. Just because.

Scientific research has shown that when you do something nice for somebody else, even walking an old person across the street, you feel better. Even your immune system, your health, gets a boost. Giving feels good. For instance, most of us enjoy giving presents even more than receiving them. Yet we often forget the benefits that come back to us through the simple act of giving. Our workplace is where we spend much of our time. It's a great place to practice acts of kindness, caring and consideration. When you offer kindness to others it will make you feel great about yourself.

Task One:

Do an "Act of Kindness" at work. It can be as simple as getting a cup of coffee for someone you normally wouldn't.

Check off when it is done

© 1999 Randy Glasbergen.

GLASBERGEN

"I'm leaving early today to have my cat neutered.
While I'm gone, select 9 people to be *Employee Of
The Month* and award each of them with a kitten."

Attitude Destination 2: China 300 A.D. **To Find: You Get Back in Life What You Put In**

In Ancient China it is said:

"Life is like a mirror. If you frown it frowns back, if you smile   it returns the greeting." —Chinese Proverb

Here, we have our own way of saying the same thing:

"Garbage in then Garbage Out." —American Proverb

Garbage in, garbage out means that if a farmer plants oat seeds, he should expect oats. If he plants wheat seeds, he shouldn't expect bananas. If we're unkind to others, we should not expect kindness back. If we're inconsiderate, we shouldn't expect consideration back. If we put out minimum effort we shouldn't expect big rewards back. Think about it—how can you expect to plant bad seeds and still get good crops?

So if you want great things out of life, then first plant some really good seeds and water them by approaching life with a great attitude.

> **Task Two:** Pick someone out at work. For at least one day treat that person far better than you have treated him or her before.

Copyright 2005 by Randy Glasbergen.
www.glasbergen.com

GLASBERGEN

"I take time to lick the customer's face, I wag my tail when they talk, I jump up and down when they walk through the door. That's what sets me apart from all the other sales people!"

Attitude Destination 3: Ancient Rome 150 B.C. **To Find: Carpe Diem**

Carpe diem," is an Ancient Latin expression that dates back 2,000 years to the Roman Empire. In English it translates to "Seize the day." It means making the most you can out of each and every day.

Not everything can be your favorite thing to do, especially at work. Making the most out of every day means you only get so many days and so many hours in life. So, make the most out of each one! Find ways to enjoy vacuuming or the tasks at work you now dread. Try it. Even your worst task can be at least a little bit enjoyable if you have the proper attitude.

> "If you don't enjoy what you already have, how can you be happy with more?" —Old Proverb

The other part of Carpe diem is valuing what you have instead of dwelling on what you don't have. At work, for instance, appreciate that you have the job and appreciate the people with whom you share the workplace.

Task Three: Pick something you dislike or even have a bad attitude towards getting done. It can be a task at work or even a task at home such as vacuuming. Do it one time making a big effort to have a positive attitude and looking for ways to enjoy that task.

© 1996 Randy Glasbergen.
www.glasbergen.com

GLASBERGEN

"I never wanted to be a seagull. I wanted to be an eagle,
but my guidance counselor was really lame."

Attitude Destination 4: Chicago School—To Visit
Marva Collins **To Find: Miracles**

Who is Marva Collins? In 1981 the world found out when a movie called *The Marva Collins Story* was released, starring Cicely Tyson. Marva Collins was a Chicago school teacher who had a belief: "There's a brilliant child locked inside every student."

Marva started her own school in a poor Chicago neighborhood. Her students were the worst inner-city students. The school system had labeled these kids dumb, disruptive or learning disabled. One child was even labeled retarded.

At the end of the first year of her school, every child scored at least five grades higher. In so doing, her school proved that the previous labels placed on these children were misguided. The CBS program, 60 Minutes, visited her school for the second time in 1996. That little girl who had been labeled as "borderline retarded" graduated from college at the top of her class.

Marva Collins method was to teach her students how to **think**, and more important, to **think for themselves.** She taught her students that when they learned to value themselves, instead of living up to the negative labels that society gave them, such as screw-up, stupid, lazy and failure—that anything was possible.

We all live our labels. When you hear yourself called something often enough, after a while you'll come to totally believe it. Then it becomes a case of **believe the label** and **live the label.**

Task Four: Think about a label holding you back the most. Such as disorganized, sloppy, lazy or shy. Do a task at work the opposite of this behavior to prove you don't have to behave like your label.

"He has issues....We're trying to build his self-esteem."

© 2000 by Randy Glasbergen.
www.glasbergen.com

GLASBERGEN

"**Forget what your mother told you—**
it's *okay* for a telemarketer to talk to strangers!"

Attitude Destination 5: Amazon Jungle Walking: **To Find:** **The Edge of Your Comfort Zone**

Jungle walking is zipping from tree-to-tree in a jungle, by dangling along wires suspended between the trees, often 100 feet above the ground. Okay, you don't have to actually do it...unless you want to. There are many other ways to find the edge of your comfort zone.

There's an expression that says, "Talk is cheap." Most of us talk a great deal about "What we're going to do," or "What we're going to change about ourselves." It's not about our words though—success and happiness are about our actions. It's what is often referred to as **"Walking the Walk."**

The thing that holds us back from making changes we need to, even if we've promised others we will make the change, is usually our comfort zone. Most people continue the same behavior that hasn't worked for them in the past, again and again because the behavior is familiar and comfortable to them.

> **Definition of Karma:** There is good karma and bad karma. Karma means whatever you do or don't do always comes back to you. Those who do good will get good; those who do bad will get bad back. You are what you do.

Changing takes work, but if you're unhappy or unsatisfied, then it probably takes a far greater effort to stay unhappy. Unhappiness takes enormous effort. There are countless hours of moaning to get done, endless time you need to spend having conversations about how miserable things are, picking just the right outfit to look unhappy in...

Task Five: Do something at work today that's outside your comfort zone, such as asking for a task you've been scared to try before, or maybe talking to someone you've been too scared to talk to.

"I'm writing about all the things I ought to do before I die. It's my oughtobiography."

Attitude Destination 5: Amazon Jungle Walking:
To Find: Taking Responsibility

Stanley "Tookie" Williams is a lesson on how someone can learn to **take responsibility** even after having done the worst acts possible and ending up on death row. Stanley Williams was one of the founders of the notorious Crips street gang in East Los Angeles. In 1979 he shot a convenience store employee to death in a robbery that netted $120.

While on death row, Stanley decided to make a difference and took a stand against street gangs, including the Crips, which he had founded. He wrote children's books telling children that there was another way of life besides gangs and he started efforts and organizations to encourage gang members to leave their gangs. Stanley received many honors for his efforts including a movie about how he turned around his life in prison, starring Jamie Foxx. He received a citation from President Bush and a nomination for the highest honor there is, the Nobel Prize for Peace. In December 2005, he was executed by lethal injection.

Taking responsibility for your life means that other people are not responsible for your success or happiness—you are. It means others aren't responsible for your mistakes and problems. Once again—you are. Even when you screw up in the biggest way imaginable, own it, and then do something to fix it—much like Stanley Williams owned up to gangs being wrong, and devoted his remaining life to fixing it.

Life Tip

You're in charge of your own life. Take responsibility. Don't let others, such as unhappy people or those messing up their own lives, bring you to their level. Take control of your own life.

If you do something wrong, admit to it—without covering it up or blaming others. If you do something wrong that affects someone else, few words are as powerful as, "I'm sorry." Learn to say "I'm sorry", and as importantly, be sincere when you do say it. Then work on the behavior that caused you to be sorry in the first place.

Task Six: : If you're like most of us, you've recently done something that you're not too proud of. Do something to take responsibility for it, even a simple thing like apologizing to someone.

Copyright 2003 by Randy Glasbergen.   www.glasbergen.com

GLASBERGEN

"**I *am* dressed for success! Of course, my idea of success may not be exactly the same as yours.**"

Attitude Destination 7: A Pet Bakery
To Find: Taking Responsibility

Many of us have a really bad habit: We take life far too seriously. Let me clear up a myth. Taking life less seriously doesn't mean being irresponsible or not being as sympathetic to others as you should be. Lots of things are serious and there are times others are counting on us to care as deeply about something as they do.

On the other hand, as hard as we try, it's scientifically impossible to worry our problems away. Think about it. What problem did you ever solve by worrying about it enough? Every problem we face falls into one of two categories: Either we can do something about it or we can't. If we can do something about it, then it seems the best strategy would be putting our energies into solving the problem, rather than putting all our energies into worrying about it. If we can't do anything about the problem, then once again it's pretty pointless to worry about something we can't change.

With most of the frustrations and problems we deal with we have a couple choices: we can **laugh about it** or **cry about it.** Sadly, the majority of people choose to cry about their problems too much of the time. This leads to unhappiness, stress and loss of energy and, to boot, misery rarely fixes the problem.

Lightening up also means not taking your problems so seriously. Everything that happens to us isn't the complete disaster we often make our problems out to be. Not every problem or argument we have with somebody is earth-shattering. Not every crisis we face is the Titanic.

Everything I learned about lightening up...I learned from my Dog

If you want a new outlook in life, try thinking like a dog. Dogs are very straightforward. If they want something, they ask. They don't know many words, so they get right to the point. If they scratch you it means pet me; if they cry, it either means let me out or give me food. What more is there to ask for in life than that? No matter how you treat your dog, even if you leave him locked up the entire day in a crate—he'll still always be happy to see you and forgive you immediately.

Very little embarrasses a dog. They are not concerned with their weight or whether their hairdo looks good. They don't require fine china to eat. A toilet bowl is as good as crystal glassware for drinking purposes. Do are not proud when it comes to what they eat. It doesn't have to be prepared by a chef. Out of the can will do just fine. A half-eaten sandwich, three-days old and found in an alley, is still a lovely treat.

Dogs expect everyone to like them, and in return they like everyone. They never have bad moods without a very good reason and they always have a smile on their face. Dogs see most situations as an opportunity to have fun. Dogs are easily entertained and don't need $90 front-row tickets in order to be amused. They put on very few airs, even when they're a pure bred. We, as their owners, know their breeding, but they don't seem to care. When it comes to sticking to something, dogs have it all over us. A dog will run to the door every time the doorbell rings—always the first to greet the person there. It doesn't matter that the person at the door is almost never there to see the dog.

Task Seven: Pick something that you have been crying or moaning about and make a joke out of it. Tell somebody the joke.

Copyright 2003 by Randy Glasbergen.
www.glasbergen.com

STRESS MANAGEMENT TECHNIQUES
1. ____
2. ____
3. ____
4. ____

GLASBERGEN

"Howl at an ambulance or fire siren every chance you get.
Run around the room in circles with a sock in your mouth.
Eat a messy meal without using your hands or utensils.
Ask a friend to scratch your belly..."

Full Day Exercise

Some things look easy to do. For instance, what could be simpler than the hula hoop? Put it around your waist and spin it. We should all be able to hula hoop for hours without missing a beat. Being happy, ecstatically happy, like spinning a hula hoop, should be simple. Just be happy. It's that easy. It should be as simple as singing the song, "Don't Worry, Be Happy" all day long. Sing that song and smile a lot. But the truth is that being happy is not easy for most people. Like spinning a hula hoop, it's a skill mastered only with a great deal of practice.

This One Day Exercise is to simply try your best to be happy for an entire day. For this one day, no matter what happens, do your very best not to react to anything negative. Don't worry about your usual problems. Smile while doing the laundry or paperwork, giggle at the grocery store. Be pleasant even when something unpleasant happens. Remember it's only one day. Try your best not to let the events of the day affect you negatively. Explain to all those around you that you are taking a happy day and that you'll fight with them, or worry about things, tomorrow.

It's a tough exercise, so just do your best. Don't beat yourself up for the moments when you slide. If you take the odd backward step, that's okay. It's like ice-skating for the first time, when you fall on your bum, say, "Ouch." Then pick yourself up and try some more.

"No matter what he tried, it was impossible for
Porky to shed his reputation for being a pig".

"You can't build a reputation on
what you are going to do."
—Henry Ford

"People who say they don't care what people think are usually desperate to have people think they don't care what people think." —George Carlin

Here's a question for you: What's the most valuable thing you own?

> A. Your Lamborghini race car, which gets you one mile down the highway in only 23 seconds
>
> B. Your 2,000-watt Stereo system, that can blast windows out of buildings 250 miles away
>
> C. Your big-screen TV set, with a picture so big that people in airplanes can watch TV at your house from 30,000 feet
>
> D. Your cat, because your cat really, really, really, really loves you!
>
> E. None of the above

The answer is "E", n**one of the above**, because the most valuable thing you own is your reputation. Your reputation is what the rest of the world thinks about you. It's the impression you give to people, and it's usually pretty true. We tend to deserve our reputations, although that's not always the case. Sometimes we just send off the wrong vibe because we don't know how to do it any differently. So if your cat really, really, really loves you, will that satisfy you if the rest of the world thinks you're a jerk?

In this chapter we will look at 20 different bad reputations, along with how to fix them—which is good! So follow me here: **Bad reputation, bad thing! Good reputation, good thing!**

As you look at these different reputations ask yourself, "Is that me? Is that what my co-workers and even the people outside the office think of me?" Most people will recognize parts of themselves in several of the 'reputations' in the next pages. Don't despair. That's normal. There are a total of 20 different bad reputations in all, so maybe just despair if you happen to be all 20. Or maybe, that just means you have your work cut out for you!

Gossiper: Anyone who starts rumors about other people whether they are true, exaggerated, or not true at all. The rule for gossip should be, **"Don't pass it on."** The gossip may not even be true. Realize that gossip hurts people—and earns the gossiper a bad reputation.

Whiner: Someone who always has something to whine about. Whiners make every issue bigger than they are. Whining has a way of making everyone feel lousy, even the whiner. Accept that life isn't always fair. Pick what you complain about carefully, and let most things slide.

Lazy: People who do the bare minimum, and sometimes not even that. They expect others to carry their load. In truth, it feels much better to know you're contributing your fair share—being respected as somebody pulling their weight. And, having lots of energy also feels great!

Irresponsible: People who don't take any responsibility for themselves, preferring to pass that on to other people. Worse, they go about doing what they do carelessly. Recognize irresponsible behavior affects others. Taking pride will make you feel good about yourself.

"Three doughnuts for me, and one for you. No, that doesn't seem fair...four for me."

Selfish: Selfish people always put their own needs first. They ask, "What's in it for me?" They either won't help or they do the minimum they can. There's an expression that says "What comes around goes around." When you help others, your payback is when others help you.

Apologize... You should be pleased to have somebody run over your foot with a Porche.

Jerks: Jerks are the ultimate inconsiderate people. Jerks actually go out of their way to see how much they can annoy, anger or frustrate. Jerks are often loud and boorish. Realize treating others in disrespectful or hurtful ways doesn't make you powerful. It makes you seem small.

"My boss treats us like a bunch of children. We'd complain, but we like the way he uses different voices when he reads us stories!"

Childish: Someone who needs constant attention, without being able to wait for a more appropriate time. They're constantly interrupting, disruptive and immature. Recognize that all of your needs can't be met the minute you have the need. Learn to respect the rights of others.

© 1999 Randy Glasbergen.

"Lemont is our finest negotiator. Perhaps you've read his book, *The Art of Pouting.*"

Manipulator: The manipulator's motto is "poor me." They may play the role of the martyr, telling others how overworked or unappreciated they are. Their major weapon is guilt. Recognize manipulation is a need to control others. Look for more positive ways to approach people.

Excuse Giver: Someone who wouldn't dream of taking responsibility for something they did. They've never made a mistake that was actually their fault. Recognize giving excuses doesn't get you off the hook. It just makes others not believe or trust you. Apologize without excuses.

Inflexibility: Inflexible people refuse to accept new ideas even exist. They like things just the way that they are. Learn to bend a bit and find a compromise—or at least deal with others in a more flexible way. Allowing for new ideas sometimes opens up the door to better ideas.

"I bit the head off one of my employees today.
Tasted like chicken."

Hotheads: Someone who often reacts with anger, when things don't go their way. Their reactions may be with hurtful words or trying to get their way through bullying. Being a hothead is a serious problem. Take time to calm down before reacting. Think, before you speak or act!

"I'd like you to keep your ears open and make
sure our office is safe from any charges of
sexual harassment. Thanks, babe."

Racist or Sexist: This is a serious problem in offices—when remarks or actions cross the border to being racist or sexist. Others often think of racists and sexists as *bigots*, an awful label to have. Nobody likes being offended. Getting along with everyone is a good habit to have.

"After calling everyone he knew a horse's behind once too often, Paul woke up one morning only to discover that the universe had played a strange joke on him."

Name Caller: People who have a label or a bad name for everyone. They make everything personal. Realize that people hate being called names. Doing so, and hurting others, makes you out to be a bully. Instead, practice being sensitive and kind in your approach.

"I like to begin every performance review with a compliment. Boy, I look good today!"

Show-off: Someone who needs to be the center of attention. They exaggerate the importance of what they do and have to say. Recognize that exaggerating your own importance doesn't impress people—it turns them off. Practice being modest and see how much better it feels.

Pessimist: A pessimist is a negative person, who sees the gloomy side of everything, and disaster around every corner. Instead of looking for ways to throw cold water on other people's ideas, get excited and optimistic. Toss your gloomy outlook and enjoy your work and life.

Inappropriate: We're all entitled to individuality, but "inappropriate people" cross the line to where their own ways of showing "their style" makes other people uncomfortable. Recognize you share the workplace with others. Appreciate there is a time to bend in order to get along.

The world descended into an ice age, while Paul took his time mulling on an important decision...what to order for lunch.

Wishy-Washy: Some people can't make a decision if their life depends on it, so they ask everyone else to decide. Recognize most decisions are not the end of the world. We all make bad decisions from time to time. Treat wrong choices as learning experiences to grow from.

"I put you on hold, you put me on hold. Everyone is holding, but nobody really feels like they're being held!"

Shy and Timid: People who are insecure, lack confidence and are often frightened of others. Fear controls their lives. They are anxious in most new situations. Being shy and timid is normal for a lot of people. Developing confidence takes time and a willingness to take risks.

"It's an interesting case alright...but I'm not sure that a judge will grant you a divorce from yourself."

Two-Faced: People who can't be trusted because you never know if they're telling the truth. They change their story constantly. Recognize that if people can't count on your honesty, then they can't count on you for very much. Relationships are built on trust. Think before you speak.

"It's a matter of your opinion...There are countries in the world where ignoring your supervisor, not following procedures, being rude to customers and co-workers, and behaving like a jerk is considered a good attitude."

'I Don't Cares': They have a bit of every bad attitude. They're not concerned with their impact on others. Wherever they go their reputation goes too, following them from job to job. Ask yourself if that is all you want from life, to be a malcontent. If not, change your attitude.

Exercise

In this section we looked at 20 different reputations you might have earned. In this exercise, consider and then write down any reputations which can sometimes be problematic for you. This is a chance to be honest with yourself.

Your Reputation Check List	
Gossiper	Inflexible
Whiner	Hothead
Selfish	Inappropriate
Jerk	Racist or Sexist
Lazy	Name Caller
Irresponsible	Show Off
Childish	Wishy-Washy
Manipulator	Shy and Timid
Excuse Giver	Two-Faced
Pessimist	I Don't Care

Techniques to Assist Change

According to the **Universal Tribunal on Changing Reputations**, (UTCR for short), there is a sure-fire technique for getting rid of a bad reputation. All you need to do is to write down the reputation on a piece of paper using a red pen, place it in a can and then set fire to it. Poof! The bad reputation is gone! But don't try it in the workplace where you can set off the sprinklers. Oh, there is one more little detail before it can work: **you have to change the behavior that earned you the reputation in the first place.**

Full Day Exercise: Pick one reputation that most applies to you. Create a plan as to how you might do things differently. Your Full-Day Exercise is to behave the opposite from your reputation for the day.

Cost to the company if you steal 10 pens: $5.00
Cost to the company if you waste 2 hours of the day: $50.00
Cost to the company if you steal the photocopier: $5,000.00
Cost to the company if you waste 2 hours a day: $5,000.00 a year.

VALUE OF A GREAT EMPLOYEE: PRICELESS

"Character is what you are,
not what you think you have."
—Marva Collins

When the World Trade Center tragedy took place, we all watched in horror and sadness. Then millions of people stood up and asked, "How can we help?" Hundreds of millions of dollars were donated in an outpouring of aid for the victims. Even children all over the world emptied piggybanks and sent their money to help. Many people gave away their vacation funds to 9/11 charities that aided victims.

Cyril Kendall was one of the people who got help. He received $190,000 in aid from the Red Cross and Safe Haven—two charitable organizations helping the families of victims. His son was killed while interviewing for a job in the World Trade Center when the planes hit the towers. Later, it was discovered that his son never existed and Cyril Kendall used this horrible tragedy as an opportunity to profit handsomely at the expense of others. He put in a false claim for nearly $200,000 simply because he thought he could get away with it!

And what about those few people who used the tragedy as an opportunity to loot stores that were part of the World Trade Center, helping themselves to a piece of diamond jewelry or some expensive electronics, while scores of people were dying? Could we have done something like that? For most of us the answer is no.

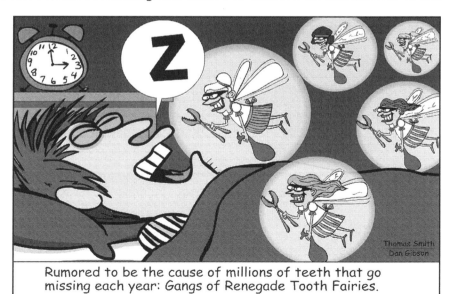

Rumored to be the cause of millions of teeth that go missing each year: Gangs of Renegade Tooth Fairies.

Here are some "Choices" to challenge you:

You're walking down the street and you spot a wallet. You pick it up. Looking inside, you see five thousand dollars. You're thinking, hmmm, what shall I do? Then you notice a library card. You realize you heard about that person on the news, a crippled woman who had lost her wallet with her life savings in it. Unable to pay rent, the crippled woman was being evicted from her home. Knowing this, what do you do with the wallet and the $5,000?

Do You Keep It ✖   **Give it Back** ✓

Maybe the story is a little different. You open the wallet and see the cash. And when you notice the driver's license, you recognize it. It's the wallet of one of the wealthiest people in the city. Now what do you do with the 5,000?

Do You Keep It ✖   **Give it Back** ✓

You're walking down a different street and you see an elderly man fall and you think he has broken his leg. Do you stop and help?

Stop to Help ✖   **Ignore the Situation** ✓

The same thing happens but this time you're late for work. You've been warned it can't happen again. Do you still stop to help?

Stop to Help ✖   **Ignore the Situation** ✓

This time you have only 30 minutes left to get to the lottery office and claim your prize of $10,000 when you see the elderly person fall and break his leg. What do you do this time?

Stop to Help ✖   **Ignore the Situation** ✓

You're at work all alone. You can sneak out of work two hours early and you won't be caught. Do you leave, knowing that you are cheating your employer?

Sneak Out ✖   **Stay At Work** ✓

Your manager commends you for the extra effort you made and an outstanding job you did on a task, and says, "This could lead to a promotion or a raise." However, it wasn't you who did that job, but someone else who is out sick that day. Do you take the credit?

Take Credit **Give the Credit to the Deserving Person**

You need some things for home and they have the items in the stockroom at work. Knowing you can save $20 by taking them and not buying them for yourself, do you take the supplies or spend your own money later at the store?

Help Yourself **Avoid the Temptation** ✓

Copyright 2002 by Randy Glasbergen. www.glasbergen.com

"I *hate* tofu sandwiches and celery smoothies, but they're the only thing my coworkers won't steal from the break room fridge!"

What is Character?

Your character is the sum total of *your values,* which help you make the difficult choices that we all face on a regular basis. For instance, how you view honesty, helping others, fairness and responsibility are all values. All of your values put together in one pile are what is known as **your integrity**.

In the next section we'll look at **Values** and the **Choices** you make.

Choice: Between Stealing or Being Honest in the Workplace

If you don't choose to be honest all of the time, then the problem becomes, "Where do you draw the line?" If it's okay to steal office supplies, then is it also okay to rob a bank? Or does the rule become, as long as you're not wearing a mask and carrying a semi-automatic weapon, then stealing is all right?

In truth, all stealing lowers the value of your character. Dishonesty has a powerful effect on us. It makes us dislike ourselves, destroys our relationships, and besides, you might get caught. Stealing can not only end a job or career, but a reputation as a thief might keep you from being hired elsewhere. Being honest, on the other hand, leads to inner peace, along with the respect and trust of others.

Francine began by stealing an office pen, but before she knew it, she had graduated to bigger stuff.

Something to Ponder

What is Your **Value** about **Honesty?** Where do you draw the line? When do you consider stealing okay?

Choice: Between Lying or Telling the Truth in the Workplace

We have an interesting way of describing our lies, with colors. There are white lies and black lies—and I suppose some people have red lies, blue lies and pink lies, to go with every outfit. White lies are little lies and black lies are the really big ones. There are probably times when we should lie a little—like to spare someone else's feelings. You probably don't want to tell a woman her baby is ugly even if you think it's the truth.

The lying that is of concern, is lying to deceive others or to gain something you're not entitled to, such as getting out of trouble for something you did. Much like stealing, lying ruins our sense of inner peace and self-worth. **Interesting fact:** The reason lie detectors work is a lie detector machine measures stress. When we are being dishonest, it puts us under stress.

After Pinocchio was let go from several jobs for excessive lying... the only work he could find was a job as a clothesline.

Something to Ponder

What is Your **Value** about **Lying?** Is it alright to lie or deceive others in order to gain an advantage or get out of trouble?

Choice: Between Putting in Little Effort or a Big Effort At Work

So why choose to go the extra mile at work and not just put yourself in cruise control and slide by?

Effort is a bit like the flour in a cake—the more flour you put into the bowl, the more cake you're going to get in return. Does effort always pay off the exact moment you make it? Not always. Sometimes you can put in your best work and nobody notices. But keep it up and they certainly will. There are so many examples we've all had in our lives that prove the value of effort. Take school—where little effort meant low marks and big effort almost always meant better grades. Effort, and the reason for making an effort, is summed up very well by Thomas Jefferson who said, "I'm a great believer in luck. I find the harder I work the more I have of it."

"The bad news is, you only have one red blood cell. The good news is, he's a workaholic!"

Something to Ponder

What is Your **Value** about **Effort?** Is it okay to slide by, doing the least you can, or would you rather go the extra mile?

Choice: Treating Others as Being Unimportant or Putting Others First

Putting others first doesn't mean putting yourself last. It means treating others as though their needs, wants, desires and opinions are equally important to your own.

It's one thing to treat others well when there is something in it for you. That means treating everyone you meet with respect, dignity and fairness, basically just as you would want to be treated. That also includes even helping people who are unlikely to be in a position to help you. There is a wonderful concept called **Pass It On** that says when you do kind deeds for others, they, in turn, will be inspired to **Pass It On** to someone else. Thus creating a world of caring, where we're all doing things for each other.

Boy Scout training manual...Adult version.

Something to Ponder

What is Your **Value** about **Treating Others?** Are you somebody who believes in **Pass It On?**

Choice: Between Closed Minded to the Ideas of Others or Being Open Minded

Here's a common misconception. Only men in suits and ties with short hair and balding heads, or women in business suits with their hair tied back in a bun are **closed-minded**—and unwilling to accept a new generation with new ideas. On the other hand, people with Mohawk haircuts are always **open-minded**.

Wrong! Often, some of the most open-minded people, willing to look at new thoughts and opinions, have buns or balding heads. Often, people with Mohawk haircuts are only open-minded to other people with Mohawks. Being open-minded means recognizing there's a place for hard rock and rap music as well as for classical and opera. Choosing to be open-minded also means leaving yourself open to consider the other guy's opinions and ideas.

"This company prides itself on being open-minded...however your idea of a 'Come to Work in Your Underwear Day' does test the limits."

Something to Ponder

What is Your **Value** about about Being **Open Minded?** Do you look at ideas that are not your own, with an open mind?

Choice: Making Others Responsible For Your Actions Or Taking Responsibility

What's the best way to move forward and advance in a job or a career? There are many factors of course, but here is one that works everywhere—taking responsibility. Taking responsibility means that if you see something that needs to get done, never leave it for the next guy—grab it! That kind of behavior gets noticed, and if you keep it up, rewarded!

Taking responsibility is also about things you should never pass on to someone else—if you want to earn respect. Don't blame your mistakes on someone else, or make excuses. Never pass on a job that's yours to do, or leave it undone, hoping the next guy will do it instead. Otherwise, the next guy gets the credit, too!

THOMAS SMITH
DAN GIBSON

"Hi I'm Tony, I'll be your waiter...I don't want to take a chance of getting your meal screwed up, so take your own darn order."

Something to Ponder

What is Your **Value** about **Taking Responsibility?** Do you pass problems on to others? Do you own your mistakes?

Choice: Between Walking Away From Failure Or Trying Harder

Is failure a good thing or a bad thing? Most people would say failure's bad, but, maybe it's not. Here's another point of view:

Failure teaches us things. Most of our valuable life lessons come from what we realize we did wrong, or could have done better. Failing is often part of the process of finding success. You might say failure is the bus we take to learning to do things better. The key question is, "How do you react when things don't go your way?" Do you quit? Or do you treat failure as a lesson? Do you quit or try some more? A Portuguese proverb says, "Stumbling is not falling." Think of your setbacks as just stumbling. What do you do when you stumble? You steady yourself and keep going. Jobs and workplaces provide plenty of setbacks or stumbles. Your best choice is to steady yourself and keep going.

Something to Ponder

What is Your **Value** about **Failure?** Are you somebody who gets discouraged and then gives up or do you keep trying?

Choice: Between Having a Good Attitude and a Bad Attitude

Most every self-help book ever written, secret to success, or greatest advice we have ever been given, usually comes to the same conclusion as to what gets us into trouble or holds us back: **Our attitude.**

Think about getting on a train. Only there are two trains heading in different directions and you have to pick which one to ride. One's heading in the direction of getting along well with other people, doing your job well, earning self-pride and the respect of others, being considerate, earning the friendship and admiration of co-workers, and succeeding because you are putting in the effort. Call it the **Good Attitude Train**. The other direction is not so good—you're thought of as lazy and disruptive, you're someone who can't be trusted or counted upon, someone who goes from job to job never getting anywhere. You can guess which train that is.

© Randy Glasbergen.
www.glasbergen.com

GLASBERGEN

"I don't like to be difficult, but it's the only thing I'm really good at!"

Something to Ponder

What is Your **Value** about **Attitude?** Which train do you choose to get on? What ways can you improve your attitude?

Life Tip

The Quality of Your Choices— Determines the Quality of Your Life

There's one other choice we also have to make: **Our Reactions**. Most of us react badly from time to time and become a little more agitated than we should, shooting off our mouth or ripping into somebody. Then we often feel badly about our reaction, when we've had a chance to think about it and cool off a bit. Or sometimes we respond to events by becoming frustrated, angry or depressed. How we react to the events in our workday, that don't go as we would like them to, is another choice we make.

You might have a problem with Reactions when...

1. The SWAT team has to be called in to deal with a hostage- taking situation, because someone took your pencil.

2. Your workplace gives everyone an extra day off. But you complain. . . out of habit.

3. Someone turns down the thermostat without asking your opinion, so you dump a bucket of ice cubes down his pants to cool him off.

4. Your supervisor asks you to stay an extra 30 minutes so you call Child Protection Services on her, claiming you're nine.

Technique: Reflect Before You React

Our reactions fall into two categorizes: they are either **Reflective** or **Reactive.** Reactive means we fire our bullets right away without thinking about who we might be shooting, or whether we really ought to be shooting them at all. Reflective means taking time to carefully consider our reactions. Then after thinking it through, deciding how to best handle the situation.

Always take 60 seconds to think—then decide how you're going to react. This will often avoid reactions you may regret later. If 60 seconds isn't enough, take 60 minutes. If 60 minutes isn't enough take 60 days. Always take the time to stop and think—then react!

64

Complaining

"Sarah's talent for complaining finally pays off."

"You can't stop the rain
by complaining."
—*Singing in the Rain*

A Fable

Big Jim Bungalow owned the largest company in the world which had 150,000 employees working in one giant building. This would have made Big Jim very happy, except for one thing—whenever he would spend time in his giant building, which was most of the time (after all, you don't get to own the world's largest company by not showing up), all he would hear everywhere, was his employee's complaining! It sounded just awful to Big Jim. If he had his choice, he would have rather been stuck in his giant building with 150,000 angry mosquitoes.

People were complaining about all kinds of things: They didn't like their jobs. Somebody else had a better job. The temperature was too hot. The temperature was too cold. Why couldn't they use softer toilet paper in the washrooms? The customers were all rotten. The supervisors were rotten. Their coworkers were all rotten. In fact, the entire world was rotten—except for them, of course. It seemed to Big Jim complaining was as much everywhere as the oxygen all the complainer's breathed...**and it made Big Jim crazy!**

Surprisingly, even after Big Jim put up a sign asking them not to complain...people still kept complaining.

Big Jim wanted a cure for all the complaining. So being Big Jim, he made a decision to take action—Big Time! Big Jim decided to assemble a Think Tank. He'd put the finest minds in the entire world together in the same room, and he wouldn't let them out until they came up with the solution to the problem. So, Big Jim found the 27 smartest people in the world. Each one had about 50 university degrees. Each had a more brilliant mind than the next one. There were sociologists and psychologists and behavioral studies experts, and some computer specialists (the very best there were), hired away from Microsoft...Oh, and there was one other person, Ralph, the office boy. Ralph had no degrees whatsoever; he hadn't even finished eighth grade. Ralph was hired because somebody said he looked pathetic: he walked on rickety legs, had glasses five inches thick. He was missing one ear, and he couldn't have been taller than four feet. But, he always seemed to be happy for some reason. Nobody could ever seem to figure out why. The 27 others were hired for their brains. Big Jim ordered them to work without stopping until they solved the problem and ended the 'complaining'. Ralph was hired to make coffee.

The first day that the 'Think Tank' started thinking, Ralph went over to the head 'really brainy person' and said, "I know what the cure is for complaining. Do you want to know what it is?" The head brainy person said to him, "We're busy being brainy. More coffee."

The 'Think Tank' thought for the next six months. Then they decided that what they needed was the world's biggest computer to help with the problem. So, they asked Big Jim for one billion dollars to purchase the colossal computer. Then they called Best Buy and ordered it. After a year of feeding in data, the computer finally spat out the solution: **'End complaining by throwing a big party, which will bring peace and harmony to the workplace.'**

Knowing that the best parties were mostly about the cake, Big Jim spared no expense and ordered 25,000 cakes. Everyone loved the party and the complaining ended. Big Jim was delighted. His team of really brainy people had found the cure for complaining: Cake! What the 'Think Tank' failed to take into consideration was that 25,000 cakes can create quite a mess. After the party ended, cake was everywhere—hanging from the walls, dripping off the sides of chairs, even clinging to toilet seats. People started asking who was going to clean up the colossal cake mess, and that's when the complaining reached its greatest volume ever. **Big Jim was about to have a stroke!**

So, the 'Think Tank' got back to work. After several more months of arguing back and forth, they decided that the problem was that the computer wasn't quite big enough. So they ordered an even bigger one, running up five billion dollars on Big Jim's credit card. The new computer was so gigantic that it took half the building just to house it. This squeezed the 150,000 employees into half their usual space, which, of course, caused the complaining to increase. Big Jim was going out of his mind! Ralph, the little office assistant with one ear and the five-inch-thick glasses once again tugged at the shirt of the head Think Tank 'really brainy guy' and said, **"I know what the cure is for complaining. Do you want to know what it is?"**

The head brainy person said to him, "We're busy here being brainy. Just bring more coffee!"

Finally, a year later, the five-billion dollar computer had a solution. Big Jim was, of course, delighted! The solution was to send everybody on a holiday. The holiday would make everyone happy. The result would surely be, no more complaining! So, 150,000 employees plus their families headed off to Hawaii in Big Jim's very large private plane. Big Jim rented all of Maui, including every hotel room. He even kicked people out of their homes as well, which caused the normally happy Hawaiians to complain. But, all that happened was people started to complain about who got the best room, the lineups for food made everyone complain something fierce—on top of sunburns and jellyfish stings.

"Turns out Big Jim had ordered 25,000 weapons of mass destruction... cleverly disguised as cake."

After the Hawaii fiasco, the problem of complaining got even more enormous! The big brains in the 'Think Tank' put their heads together and decided that what they needed to really tackle a problem of this enormous size was—you guessed it—an even bigger computer.

When you have a bigger problem to solve, what you need is a bigger computer.

The new computer was the size of a shopping mall, plus 10 football fields. The computer had one trillion Megs of RAM, a three-gazillion Meg hard drive, and an eight-billion decibel quadraphonic sound system guaranteed to blow the roofs off of houses two continents away. Oh, and they threw in a DVD player too. The computer occupied three-quarters of the building. This really squeezed people tight, causing them to stand on each other's shoulders just to work. This created complaining that was off the charts. Big Jim went out of his mind! He was miserable! Once again, Ralph said politely, **"Excuse me, but I know what the solution is. I know what the cure is for complaining. Does anyone want to know what it is?"**

This time it was the computer that said to him, "I'm busy here being brainy. More coffee!"

Then one morning a few months later the computer spit out a request: "In order to solve this problem of everyone complaining, please make me into an even bigger computer."

Big Jim asked, "How am I going to do that? People are on top of each other as it is. There won't be any space left for anyone."

The computer answered, "Precisely. Fire them all! That is the solution to ending the complaining."

So, Big Jim, not being able to stand the complaining another second, fired them all. Once they all left, including all the really brainy people in the 'Think Tank', Big Jim found himself alone with his gigantic computer. Except for one other person, the last person of the 150,000 employees in Big Jim's really big company to leave. Standing on a stepladder to shut off the lights, Ralph turned to Big Jim and said, "I know what the cure for complaining is, besides firing everyone."

Sadly, Big Jim no longer owned the world's largest company. He resolved to never have people work for him ever again. Having decided to start a new business selling products to hermits, Big Jim turned to the four-foot-tall, one-eared office boy with the rickety legs, and asked, "Okay, tell me. What is it that will cure complaining?"

To which Ralph answered, **"Appreciation will."**

The moral of the story is: Sometimes 4-foot-tall guys with 5-inch thick glasses and one ear…know what they're talking about.

And I bet you thought that after five pages and four cartoons the answer would be something really spectacular, something better than just **"appreciation."** The truth is, nothing is better (at least for ending complaining) than appreciation. In this section you'll hopefully find out why.

Do You Appreciate What You Have?

No matter what we achieve, it's built into our human nature to want more. We all live in the lap of luxury compared to how even the richest people lived 100 years ago. **Yet it's not nearly enough.**

Too often, the things we don't yet have are what we desire most. We often have the bad habit of placing the greatest value on those items we don't have because we assume our happiness would skyrocket if we had them. On the other hand, we don't put nearly enough value on things we already do have.

Do you appreciate your family and friends enough? What about your job and your coworkers? Do you value the natural-born gifts you've been given, such as the ability to paint, sing or crack a joke? When you sing the "National Anthem", is it just words or do you value your country?

Appreciation is one of those rare words that has magical powers to transform life into a happier place. Like the air which we breathe, without appreciation, the good things we have suffocate. In almost every relationship, appreciation is the fertilizer making it grow. Without appreciation, everything loses its luster or dies. Lack of appreciation destroys happiness and lives. It destroys marriages and families and it even destroys jobs and careers.

A Joke About Appreciation

Some jokes are not only funny but teach lessons. Here's one:

A woman sat on the beach with her grandson who was building a sandcastle. Suddenly, a huge wave came in and swept the boy out to sea. The grandmother was understandably horrified and, not knowing what else to do, she threw herself to her knees and started pleading with the heavens, "I've been a kind woman my entire life. I've done nothing but good deeds for others. I've never asked for anything before. I beg of you, please return my grandchild to me!"

Suddenly another huge wave hits the beach and back sweeps the boy. He is scared, but completely unharmed. The woman comforts her grandson, and then turns her head to the heavens and comments, "He had a hat."

Why Do We Find So Much to Complain About?

It boils down to this: The reason we complain is usually because of our focus. Our focus is constantly on the things that we don't have, as well as our needs that aren't being met, and not focusing on **'appreciating'** what we do have.

> *"I used to worry about having no shoes to walk,*
> *but then I met a man with no feet."*
> —Anonymous Quote

Did You Know

Liberia, a country on the west coast of Africa, has the highest unemployment rate in the world: 85%. This means only 1 out of every 7 people even has a job. Those who are working earn an average of $3.19—but not per hour—that's what they earn for a day. Over a third of people in Liberia earn less than $1.00 a day. It's no wonder the average life expectancy in Liberia is only 42 years. **Makes you appreciate your job more, doesn't it?**

Copyright 2007 by Randy Glasbergen.
www.glasbergen.com

"Please hold for the next customer service agent.
This call may be recorded to play back to
your mother if you use bad words."

Appreciation List

We all have plenty of things to complain about and plenty of other things to appreciate. In most cases, such as with our jobs, family or friends, we can find both things to complain about and things we can appreciate. Whichever we do, **complain** or **appreciate**, is a matter of choice. The best way to enjoy life is to constantly remind yourself, not of the things that are wrong with your job or your life, but with what's right and can be **appreciated**.

Create an **Appreciation List**, then tear out the page and keep it with you. Add to the lists as you come up with more items to appreciate. Read it often, especially in those moments when you are feeling the most frustrated in your job, your life, or with the people in your life.

	Things I Have in My Life I Appreciate
1	Sunshine and the gorgeous weather
2	My good health
3	Supportive co-workers
4	Friendships I enjoy
5	
6	
7	
8	
9	
10	

Full Day Exercise: Practice appreciating others. Pay at least 5 compliments and make a point of letting people who do things for you know that you appreciate and value.

Because of his ongoing ability
to increase office productivity,
the "Employee Of The Month" award
again goes to Mr. Coffee.

"It's not the job you do — It's
how you do the job."
—Source Unknown

Why Rules Are Needed

To get things done in an effective and efficient way, everyone needs to be on the same page, or in sports terms, playing the same game. Imagine a football game where each of the players ran a different play at the same time. It wouldn't work, would it? Or imagine two cooks sharing a bowl. One's trying to mix a cake in the bowl and the other's breading chicken. The result. . . bad cake and bad chicken! Rules are how we all are able to function together for a **common purpose—on the job that means the mission of your workplace.**

"Don't take these if you are nursing, pregnant, or about to become pregnant."

RULE ONE: Listen to Supervisors

In every workplace they are called something different: Supervisors, managers, team leaders and bosses are the most common titles. Going back to the example of the football game, where everyone needs to be running the same play at the same time—somebody needs to be the one to decide what the best play to run is. Even though teamwork is encouraged, **somebody needs to be in charge.**

People with authority have to enforce rules, which is not always to everyone's liking. Most supervisors try their hardest to do their job as best they can, trying to meet everyone's needs, answer to their bosses, address budgets, while trying to organize a group of people into an effective team. So Rule One is to give your supervisors credit, too. Their job is not always easy.

> *"No one ever listened themselves out of a job."*
> —Calvin Coolidge, USA President

Job Tip The best way to get along with a supervisor, boss or manager is by **treating them with respect.**

Life Tip The best way to get along with **anyone** at all is by **treating them with respect.**

RULE TWO: Try Not to Miss Work

Careerbuilder.com surveyed managers to ask some of the worst reasons they'd heard for missing work. Among the reasons were:

1. Employee was poisoned by his mother-in-law

2. A buffalo escaped from the game reserve and kept charging the employee every time she tried getting into her car

3. Employee broke his leg snowboarding off his roof while drunk

4. Employee's dog swallowed her bus pass

5. Employee was feeling the symptoms of his pregnant wife

When you don't go to work because you feel just a bit ill, too tired, or you just don't feel like it, you're letting lots of people down—your supervisors, your coworkers, who'll probably have to work that much harder to make up for your absence—and most especially, yourself.

When others can't depend on you, you lose their trust as well. Even if a lion actually did eat your keys, and the zookeeper advised letting the lion keep them, be dependable.

Copyright 2003 by Randy Glasbergen.
www.glasbergen.com

GLASBERGEN

"Of course you can take paid parental leave when
your cat has her kittens...but you'll have to
prove that you're the father."

RULE THREE: Don't be Late for Work

Be dependable. Being on time to work is a matter of preparing properly, figuring out the time you need to get ready to leave for work, then deciding how long it will take you to get to work. When you do this, don't assume everything will happen perfectly. Allow for the fact that traffic is often slower than you planned or buses can be missed by a matter of seconds. Give yourself extra time by planning to be at work 10 or 15 minutes early, just in case something unexpected happens. Most of us have the temptation in the morning to sleep a few minutes extra. But, resist that snooze button!

Careerbuilder.com surveyed managers to ask some of the worst reasons they'd heard for being late to work. Among the reasons were:

1. I dreamed I was fired, so I didn't bother getting out of bed

2. I had to take my cat to the dentist

3. I got all the way to the office and realized I was still in my pajamas, so I had to go home and change

4. I saw you weren't in the office, so I went out looking   for you

5. I ran over a goat

Being late more than occasionally makes a statement about who you are. Much like being absent does, being late puts an unfair burden on your coworkers because they have to pick up the slack until you get there. It also labels you as someone who can't be responsible or trusted, and that holds you back.

THOMAS SMITH
DAN GIBSON

SUPERVISOR

"Normally I would consider 'Abducted by Aliens' to be a pretty farfetched excuse for missing work, however in this case..."

RULE FOUR: Ask!

For some reason, many people shy away from asking questions. We'd rather take days working out a problem ourselves, than ask for help. We have a false idea that if we ask someone questions it will paint us as a dummy who can't figure things out for ourselves.

When you just start a new job, it usually takes lots of questions to be able to understand your job. Without asking questions it might take weeks to learn important information on your own, that you might have learned in a few minutes by asking. Never be afraid to ask as many questions as you need to. Sometimes you even have to repeat the same question more than once, because we don't always understand the answer the first time. That's normal, so never be embarrassed to repeat a question until you understand.

Many people fear asking a stupid question as though asking a stupid question would rub off on them, like a horror movie: ***The Attack of the Stupid Questions.*** The moment you ask a stupid question, then poof, you become stupid! In truth, **there are no stupid questions** when it comes to understanding what's important to know.

"At first he thought it was a stupid question...then Russell thought about it some more...what is a bald guy supposed to put down as his hair color?"

RULE FIVE: Be Patient

Being patient is about not letting yourself get frustrated, even though in most work-places there's plenty to be frustrated about. On occasion, we all do get frustrated. Here's something that may help: It's a technique we first learned a long time ago called a time-out. If you thought time-outs were just for 3-year-olds, you're wrong! When 3-year-olds become frustrated, nothing calms them down like a time-out does. When you need to, take a few minutes during a work break and take a time-out. A time-out is a quiet time to calm yourself to rebalance your perspective.

"I need you to write a manual to interpret the brochure that we created to clarify the pamphlet that we printed to define the handout that we sent to explain the memo."

RULE SIX: Get Along With Others

Rule Six is another rule most of us learned when we were very young, maybe in the first few weeks of kindergarten. It's how to get along with others, or what our mothers called, **"Playing nice."**

There are many common sense rules to getting along, including being nice, consideration, sharing, not calling someone names or being insulting, and being respectful of others. The same ways in which children get along with each other, also applies to adults. What we don't have is a kindergarten teacher to remind us of these valuable lessons we may now have forgotten.

Technique

Most of the time when people don't get along it's because they have different agendas. For instance, one person wants the temperature turned up and the other wants it turned down. It's not a case of either person being right or wrong. They just have different ways of looking at the same situation. **Getting Along** always begins with the understanding that someone else has a different way of seeing the same thing and then taking a few seconds to consider their point of view. When you consider someone else's point of view it is much more likely that they'll be willing to consider yours. Once you both see each other's side of things, **Compromise** can happen.

"I understand you were all sent here for a refresher course in playing nice."

RULE SEVEN: Leave what's Outside Work, *Outside!*

Think of work, and your life outside of work, as being similar to a Tupperware container that has two compartments. After all, the mashed potatoes are not meant to mix with the meat. It's difficult for people to separate their work life and their life outside of work completely. And sometimes it does happen—a little bit of the mashed potatoes mixes in with the meat. Sometimes you need to deal with a personal matter when you're at work, or you have a personal problem on your mind that you can't shake. Other times you might bring a problem from your job home, or work home to do. To be fair to your workplace, when you're at work, try your best to focus your attention on just your job.

Know your workplace's policy on dealing with personal matters such as phone calls during work hours. Try to keep calls as short as possible, and restricted to matters that can't wait until after work or a break.

One of the best ways to deal with a personal problem is getting your mind off it for a while. When we think about the same problem continuously, it not only wears us down, but we lose our ability to see the problem, and the solution, clearly. **Focusing on your work helps in solving your personal problems!**

RULE EIGHT: Care About Jour Job

Backing your company or workplace is very much like supporting your local sports team. Only you're actually part of the team, so you get to be part of the reason they succeed. When your workplace has problems, you can add to the problem, making the situation worse—or you can be part of the solution, making it better. Your workplace deserves your loyalty.

Understanding the 'Law of Reciprocity'

The **Law of Reciprocity** means we tend to get back exactly what we put in. *You reap what you sow.* It's true! If you put a lot into something, you're far more likely to get a lot back. If you put only a little in, don't expect to get much back. The **Law of Reciprocity** states:

> "You'll get back from your job exactly what you're prepared to put into your job."

RULE NINE: Take Care of Yourself

Take care of the personal habits that will make you a better team member, such as eating properly for maximum energy. Also, watch your health so that you don't get sick, and maybe get others sick as well. Most importantly, try to get enough sleep so that you don't constantly feel like napping on the job.

"Lose some weight, quit smoking, move around more and eat the carrot."

RULE TEN: Follow All Other Rules & Procedures

You mean there are more rules? Yes, every company has its own set of rules and procedures. They have been designed over time to make the company flow the best. Understand and value the fact that there are good reasons behind each rule and procedure.

"Memo, re: Casual Dress Code on Fridays.
1) Sandals are permitted, but not with black socks.
2) No bare midriffs for men over 40.
3) Ties are optional, but may not be worn as a loin cloth.
4) Donuts were not meant to be worn as a hat..."

"Excellence is doing a common thing in an uncommon way."
—Booker T. Washington

The Secret of Success

I am about to give you **the real secret of success** in any job or career—not that other things aren't important, too. Of course other things play a part in success, such as how well you cooperate with people, and your overall attitude and mood—but there is **one word** or **one habit** that matters more than anything else. It will make all the difference in the world as to whether you're successful or not.

And do you know what that one word or habit is?

Guess. . .

Copyright 2002 by Randy Glasbergen.   www.glasbergen.com

No, that's not it—it's not making money. I'm going to whisper the word very softly, because it's a very powerful word and we wouldn't want this secret word to lead to absolutely everyone being successful, would we? So here it is...

Actually, **I can say this secret to success word loudly**, because there's plenty of opportunity for success to go around for everyone. The word is. . .

93

Effort!

> "Life is a 10-speed bicycle. Most of us have gears we never use." —Charles Shultz, *Peanuts*

So Why Make the Effort?

Because making an effort usually leads to success. Think of success as being like a beach. A beach feels sunny and warm. Everybody is happy when at the beach. Success feels just the same way.

What is success? Many people make the mistake of thinking that success has something to do with money. Success often leads to more money, but it is very different from being rich. Success is when you feel a sense of contentment from living your life the best way you know how and from being an example to others to do the same. Success happens when you have created a nice balance in your life between pleasure, relaxation, friendships, family, health and work. Think back to the **Law of Attraction:** You attract success by having a positive attitude toward succeeding. **The Law of Reciprocity** says the more you put into being successful, then the more success you get back in return. This is where effort comes in. **Effort is the main ingredient in success.**

And success tends to bring other rewards as well...

Making an effort in the present...Can make life ever so pleasant!

Going to the Beach: *THE GAME*

Let's play a video game called "**Going to the Beach**". In this game there'll be **stops** you need to **make** in order to **Get to the Beach** and other **stops** you need to **avoid**. What do you win for playing? *Success!* Are you ready to play?

So how do you begin heading in a direction of more success and happiness from your job, or for that matter, from anything else? How do you **Get to the Beach?** It begins with one word: **Start!**

All video games have two components—tools to energize you and help you win the game, and the bad stuff, the things that destroy your energy and success, the stuff to avoid. *Let's begin with the things to avoid.*

1. Avoid Being Mediocre

Otherwise known as second-rate, run-of-the-mill, so-so, uninspired and barely passable. Something that's below standard, that slides by, but isn't very good. **Making it to the Beach and Being Successful** are about making the kind of effort that makes you first-rate and inspired, and helps you be top notch in your job. Something to think about: When you're being mediocre, and if that's all that you expect of yourself, who are you really cheating?

© Randy Glasbergen.
www.glasbergen.com

"For what it's worth, this is some of the finest substandard mediocrity I've ever seen."

2. Avoid Slacking Off

Most people are basically honest; they certainly wouldn't consider stealing something like a copy machine worth $5,000. Yet if you slack off for 2 hours a day, it amounts to the same thing, costing your workplace thousands of dollars a year in time you wasted.

Let's say you went to the store and bought a pie. Then when you got home and took the pie out of the box, you discovered one of the pieces was missing. How would you feel? Ripped off? When you slack off, then your workplace gets a pie with a missing piece. How fair is that to them? People who put in a steady effort all the time are like a pie with all the pieces. And that leads to success.

> "No rule of success will work if you don't."

3. Avoid Making Excuses

Some people work much harder at thinking up excuses than they do working at getting the job done. Making excuses is almost a surefire way to never Make it to the Beach. In the workplace we use excuses to push the blame for our actions onto someone else, as a way to avoid a task we don't really want to do or we make excuses to avoid getting into trouble.

When you make excuses, you pay for it later, because people stop believing anything you say. Even worse, you lose their respect and your own self-respect. Then the one time you really do have a valid excuse, nobody believes you.

You Might Have an Excuse Problem When...

1. Your dog ate the work you took home to complete, ate your pants making you late, then ate your keys causing you to miss work altogether. . . and you don't even own a dog.

2. It's the sixth time this year you've had to go to your grandma's funeral, leading your supervisor to comment, "The woman just won't stay dead."

3. You weren't at work because your cat was having kittens, and your cat's name is Bob.

4. Avoid Tired Thoughts

Here's an interesting experiment. Say to yourself, "I'm feeling itchy," and see what happens. Even reading the word 'itchy' will make most people feel the need to scratch themselves.

Our thoughts tell us how to behave. So, if you have tired thoughts that'll make you more tired. So don't say to yourself, "I'm tired," or "I need a nap." Instead use energized words. Tell yourself, "I'm feeling energetic!" or peppy, or zingy!

5. Avoid Needing Instant Gratification

We live in an instant gratification society where you can make a cup of coffee in 45 seconds, watch people become millionaires on a 60-minute television show, watch other people become multi-millionaires in a 30-second lottery drawing, while eating fast-food. We want our success or our rewards to happen instantly, and we get very frustrated when they don't! The problem is that workplaces are typically not instant gratification places. You work for a week or two before you get paid. Learning the ropes of anything new takes time, and rewards come slowly. M**aking it to the beach** and **success** take time. A workplace is not fast food. Work and effort come now, and then the good things, the rewards we get from work—the money we receive, raises, vacations, promotions, recognition—all come later.

INSTANT GRATIFICATION ACCOUNTING DEPTARTMENT

"Ok, I've worked another five minutes...pay me a dollar."

6. Avoid Unrealistic Expectations

Who is Takeru Kobayashi? He's the six-time winner of the Nathan's Hot Dog Eating Competition, considered the Super Bowl of competitive eating. In 2006, he broke his own world record by eating 54 hotdogs in 12 minutes. He also holds a world record in hamburger eating, 67 burgers in 8 minutes. Takeru even had a hotdog eating competition against a Kodiak bear. The bear out-ate him 36 dogs to Takeru's 31. Even more amazing, Takeru, who routinely takes on professional eaters twice his weight, not to mention bears, weighs only 144 pounds!

Sometimes people are capable of doing the unrealistic. Most of us, most of the time, are not. If you set a goal of beating Takeru's hotdog eating record by next week, or ever, could you do it? If you're like me, or even eat hotdogs at all, 3 would be about it, much less 54. Can you run a marathon, 26 miles, next month, if you've never even jogged before? Can you get a promotion right away, or add 50% to your salary? Or get a job done that you've left to the last minute, in half the time it
takes?

Being Successful is achieved when you have a realistic plan. This means accepting that achieving goals, such as getting promotions or salary increases, takes time. It's also unrealistic to expect that there won't be disappointments along the way.

THOMAS SMITH
DAN GIBSON

"I wanted to put hard work to the test, so I worked at an unbelievable pace, sacrificing myself, practically working myself into the grave, constantly giving it my all...But I didn't sell a house, get a listing, nothing...I can only conclude, hard work doesn't pay off. That had to be the toughest 3 hours of my life."

> *"The only job where you start at the top is digging a hole."*

5. Avoid Sabotaging Yourself

Sometimes it happens that everything is going your way—and then suddenly it bites you in the butt. A job has never gone better. Then you do something to really screw it up. It's human nature for a lot of people. It's as though they can't handle life when it's going too well. They just have to do something to mess it up!

So what causes people to sabotage themselves, either right out of the gate or even when things are going, well, almost too good? Partly it's a voice deep inside that says, "I don't deserve good things to happen to me." Partly, it's when good judgment breaks down and common sense goes out the door. Other times you start out great, and then drift back to being the same old you. This is what's called a *bad pattern*.

Technique To Try

Think about any sabotaging patterns you have and what is getting you in trouble. Complete this sentence. ***I sabotage myself when...***

To solve the problem, you must break the pattern. Forgive yourself for that which happened in the past. Today is a fresh day, a new chance. Resist. When you feel yourself going back to old patterns, fight it. Tell others what you're doing, form a support team.

THE DAY ALL THE MISSING SOCKS CAME BACK.

99

> ## *"It's not the job you do, it's how you do the job."*

Now that we've discussed 7 things to avoid, let's get to the good stuff, the **Stops** along the road to M**aking it to the Beach**, or **Success** in your job. Success at work is bound to rub off on all the other parts of your life as well—so, **4 stops** and then the Beach**.**

1. Clarity

Clarity is when you clearly understand your job, and as important, what doing a great job even looks like. When people aren't doing the best job they can, it's often because they don't understand what's expected of them or what more is needed for them to excel. Most jobs are full of confusion, which brings us back to ask questions. Ask your supervisor, or even coworkers what you can do in order to do a superb job.

© 1998 Randy Glasbergen.
www.glasbergen.com

GLASBERGEN

"Thank you for calling Creative Business Seminars.
If you'd like to become a more creative problem solver,
press 1 without touching any part of your telephone."

Technique: Modeling

Let's say you wanted to get better at golf. The best person to show you how would be Tiger Woods, the world's best golfer. Even by watching TV you can see how Tiger Woods hits a golf ball. Copy him and then get better yourself. That's modeling. To get really great at your job, pick out someone else who's superb at a similar job, and model what they do and how they go about doing it. You can even model someone who gets along well with others, to learn that skill. **To be successful, model success!**

> *"Enthusiasm is contagious. You could start an epidemic."*

2. Enthusiam

Enthusiasm is like the gas in a car's tank. You can go a long ways with just your enthusiasm. Even if you are new to a job and don't know how to do it well, or you're not the best at something, a lot of enthusiasm will make up for a lack of talent. No matter what job you're in, whether you're dealing with customers or just coworkers, people respond to enthusiasm! Not just that, but you enjoy everything you do much more when you're enthusiastic!

So what is enthusiasm exactly? It's allowing yourself to get excited, show interest, be devoted, do something with feeling behind it, or zeal. Stop 2 is showing this enthusiasm for your job!

Even after years on the job...Max had never lost his enthusiasm for sewage!

3. Patience

Rewards will come to you in time when you keep your best effort flowing. Sometimes the positive things you do don't get noticed right away, but keep it up—no good deed goes unanswered in the long run. Think of a toddler learning to walk—the first few attempts may lead nowhere. Practice patience. You may not see success right away, but you'll get there!

© 1997 Randy Glasbergen.

"Dave, if you can earn the company an extra 500 million dollars by noon today, I'll let you keep half."

4. Self-Discipline

Has this ever happened to you? You don't feel like doing something that you ought to because doing something fun, or something that doesn't take thought or energy, is so much easier? The final stop before **Success** or **Making it to the Beach** is knowing it takes self-discipline to succeed at anything. If you've ever played a musical instrument, it's all about practice, practice, practice. Success isn't something you just show up for, and there it is. However you define success in your job, you have to work at it. Self-discipline is working at something even when it's tough or you don't feel like doing it. It means having a great attitude when it's easier to have a bad one.

Copyright 2002 by Randy Glasbergen. www.glasbergen.com

"Do I get partial credit for simply having the courage to get out of bed and face the world again today?"

"To connect with our younger employees, you need to be more like Ozzy Osbourne. If you're not willing to bite the head off a bat, would you bite the head off a chocolate bunny?"

"There is music wherever there is harmony."
—Thomas C. Halliburton

What "Death Row" Can Teach Us About Work

The following are excerpts from the memoirs of **Luis Ramirez**, from his first day on **Death Row in 1999**. He was executed in 2005.

It's Titled Brown Paper Bag

"I'm about to share with you a story whose telling is long past due. It's a familiar story to most of you reading this from death row. And now it's one all of you in "free world" may learn from. It's the story of my first day on the row.

I was placed in a cell on H-20 wing over at the Ellis Unit in Huntsville, Texas. A tsunami of emotions were going through my mind at the time. I remember the only things in the cell were a mattress, pillow, a couple of sheets, a pillow case, a roll of toilet paper, and a blanket. I remember sitting there, utterly lost.

The first person I met there was Napoleon Beasley. Back then, death row prisoners still worked. His job at the time was to clean up the wing and help serve during meal times. He was walking around sweeping the pod in these ridiculous looking rubber boots. He came up to the bars on my cell and asked me if I was new. I told him that I had just arrived on d/r. He asked what my name is. I told him, not seeing any harm in it. He then stepped back where he could see all three tiers. He hollered at everyone, "There's a new man here. He just drove up. His name is Luis Ramirez."

When he did that, I didn't know what to make of it at first. I thought I had made some kind of mistake. You see? Like most of you, I was of the impression that everyone on d/r was evil. I thought I would find hundreds of "Hannibal Lecters in here. And now they all knew my name. I thought "Oh well, that's strike one." I was sure that they would soon begin harassing me. This is what happens in the movies after all.

Well, that's not what happened. After supper was served, Napoleon was once again sweeping the floors. As he passed my cell, he swept a brown paper bag into it. I asked him "What's this"? He said for me to look inside and continued on his way. Man, I didn't know what to expect. I was certain it was something bad. Curiosity did get the best of me though. I carefully opened the bag. What I found was the last thing I ever expected to find on death row, and everything I needed. The bag contained some stamps, envelopes, notepad, pen, soap, shampoo, toothpaste, tooth brush, a pastry, a soda, and a couple of Ramen noodles. I remember asking Napoleon where this came from.

He told me that everyone had pitched in. That they knew that I didn't have anything and that it may be a while before I could get them. I asked him to find out who had contributed. I wanted to pay them back. He said, "It's not like that. Just remember the next time you see someone come here like you. You pitch in something."

I sat there on my bunk with my brown paper bag of goodies, and thought about what had just happened to me. The last things I expected to find on death row was kindness and generosity. I thought of how many times I had seen "good people" of the world, pass by some man, woman, or child holding a sign that read, "Hungry," or "Will work for food." I'm guilty of the same. I just passed them by. By the end of the block, or upon reaching my destination that poor, hungry, tattered, and perhaps dirty, soul had been forgotten. Lost among my daily challenges and struggles with life. Yet, here on death row among the worst of the worst, I didn't have to hold up a sign. They knew what I needed and they took it upon themselves to meet those needs.

What's in the brown paper bag? I found caring, kindness, love, humanity, and compassion of a scale that I've never seen the "good people" in the free world show towards one another.

Luis Ramirez
999309 Polunsky Unit
3872 FM 350
South Livingston, Texas 77351, USA

Cooperation

How does a work environment function best? The same way a family, a club, or even a Death Row cell block does—with cooperation. Cooperation means people looking out for one another, helping where they can. It's somebody boosting a car for someone when their battery is dead, offering a ride home, or a cup of coffee if you're heading to the coffee room anyway. Cooperation is considering someone else's needs and feelings.

How Our Behavior Impacts Others

The ultimate form of cooperation is kindness. Kindness is any act of caring that tells someone else, whether it's someone close to you or a complete stranger, that they count. **Kindness** is the ultimate **Pass It Along** gesture. When you are kind to others, it encourages them to be kind to someone else. **Pass it on** works well for acts of kindness—but, unfortunately, it works just as well for unkindness too. So, like a cold or the flu, if you're in a lousy mood you can pass that on to your coworkers, too. If you're tired or frustrated, chances are you'll make someone else tired or frustrated. Get angry at someone and what happens? They often get angry right back. Then there are two angry people and before you know it, an entire epidemic of angry people breaks out. Most of us wouldn't think of sneezing into someone's face. Yet we'll come to work with a sour mood, and not think twice about infecting others with our bad mood.

The Golden Rule

We've all heard it a million times. It's such an important rule that it even gets its own color. No other rule gets a color! **The Golden Rule: Treat others the way you'd like them to treat you.**

Different Agendas

There's a reason why my favorite ice cream shop has 31 flavors—because we do not all like the same flavor. Some of us love Rum Raisin and others don't—but the Heavenly Hash is well, heavenly.

We wouldn't call someone "wrong," for having a different favorite flavor of ice cream than our own. We recognize there's no right or wrong flavor of ice cream—just different people with different opinions on ice cream. So then, why do we believe that when people have different opinions on more important topics it means—somebody has to be right and somebody else wrong?... Instead of merely being different people with different points of view?

The question is, "If we all liked the same flavor, what would that flavor be?"

In the Broadway play Fiddler on the Roof two men got into a heated argument over whether what was sold to one man was a horse or a mule. They took their problem to Tevye, the wisest man in the village. He listened to the first man's story and after hearing his side Tevye said, "You're right." Then the second guy said, "Wait a minute. You haven't heard my side," and so he told his. After listening to the second man's side, Tevye said, "You're right." So both men turned to Tevye and protested, "We can't both be right!" To which Tevye thought for a moment, then replied, "You're right."

Too often we spend a great deal of energy trying to convince someone else we're right. Instead, respect that two people can see things differently, and they can both be right!

Two views of the same cat.

Age Differences

In any workplace, people of all ages work side-by-side. The key to harmony between different age groups is respect. There is plenty that both age groups can gain from each other. Older workers have a great deal of practical wisdom from many years of experience to share with younger workers. Younger workers often have a superior knowledge of newer technology they can share.

111

Different People Have Different Skills

Different people have varying degrees of skills when it comes to specific tasks. Some of us are mechanical whizzes and can take something apart and put it right back together again. Others can barely figure out screwing in a light bulb. Some people can write well—while others can't. We all have different strengths and weaknesses. Take technology, for instance. In many workplaces, computers and other technology are constantly changing. For some people this is no problem. Others are easily baffled. Don't criticize or get frustrated. Lend your assistance and be patient. Some people are frightened of change. Remember, **Pass It On**.

Cultural Differences

Workplaces have a rainbow of different people representing many different cultures from around the world. You might have been born in the city where you work, or maybe you were born halfway across the world. The person working beside you on one side may be from Nigeria and the person on the other side from India or Korea. Think of it this way: That's what makes a workplace so rich—different cultures sharing their traditions and heritage.

There are challenges. Different cultures have different ways of viewing the same situation. Respect these different ways of thinking. There's no right or wrong, just different viewpoints. The key is to be respectful and careful not to offend. People are entitled to live according to their own cultural upbringings, and the different values taught them—just as you are.

Language Difference

One of the main challenges many people have is language. It's important to under-stand that many people did not grow up speaking English. Respect them for taking on the challenge of learning a new language considered one of the most difficult to learn.

Did You Know

English isn't the most spoken language in the world—it's Number 4! More people speak Mandarin, Arabic and Spanish than English. Here's an interesting question: Take a guess on how many languages are spoken by at least 1 million people in the world? Some of the languages include Bengali (171 million people speak it), Telugu (66 million), Azeri (30 million), Igbo, Shona, and Sinhala. The answer is that there are 251 languages spoken by at least 1 million people.

Copyright 2000 by Randy Glasbergen.

"Our goal is to establish language that is gender-neutral, ethnic-neutral, and age-neutral while celebrating our spirit of diversity."

Individuality

Not only are we different because we come from so many varying cultures, we're dif-ferent because each one of us is an individual. In expressing our own individuality, sometimes people can go too far! Be careful not to cross the boundary to where you offend other people or are a problem for your workplace, in dealing with more conser-vative coworkers and customers. Express yourself, you should! But getting along also means that sometimes you have to give a little too, in order to fit in.

Famous Moments in Braces: As a 12 year old girl, Martha Stewart gets her braces.

Men and Women

There are 251 languages and cultures to deal with in a workplace, yet sometimes the groups that have the hardest time getting along are men and women—even though there are only 2 genders! According to numerous books on the subject, when men and women look at the same situations, they often see them differently. Getting along comes down to that all important word, **respect.**

There is one other important aspect to the relationship between men and women in the workplace: ***boundaries.*** In the workplace the word boundary means a line that you never cross. If you have the tiniest doubt that something you say or do could cross the boundary, then the answer is **don't do it!**

1. Boundaries include any remarks, including comments or jokes, that could be **offensive** to any member of the opposite sex. That means anything that could be taken as either sexual in nature or as a put-down of the opposite sex.

2. Boundaries include touching of any kind that could be taken as sexual in nature, as a come-on, or in any way.

3. Boundaries include asking for sexual favors of any kind, including even a date, in exchange for something you can do for someone else in the workplace. Once again, ***don't do it!***

One other important thing—never allow yourself to be the victim of sexual harassment. You have rights to your boundaries. Report any incident to someone of authority.

Personal Space

Getting along with your coworkers also means respecting a variety of boundaries. People are entitled to their personal space, so don't enter someone else's area, go into their locker, or borrow/take things that belong to someone else, without asking. People are also entitled to the privacy of their thoughts, so don't pressure someone to talk about something they don't want to, unless it is important to your job that you know.

Other Boundaries

© Randy Glasbergen, 1997.
www.glasbergen.com

GLASBERGEN

"Sorry about the odor. I have all my
passwords tattooed between my toes."

Let's face facts—some of us have certain habits that annoy others or hygiene issues that offend others. You're part of a community in a workplace. You might not notice your own odor if you haven't showered in three days, but others do. Come to work showered, in clean clothes, with your teeth brushed and wearing deodorant. It's common courtesy to others.

Consider what habits you have that annoy coworkers. If one or two people have said something about it to you in the past, then it's probably a bad habit. For instance, not covering your mouth when you sneeze is a bad habit. Not cleaning up after yourself in your area, or a public area such as a restroom, tends to annoy others who see or share this area. Singing while you're working may be nice for you, but your coworkers might not consider the workplace a karaoke bar. Consider your habits and how they impact others!

> **You might have a problem with offending people when...**
>
> 1. People know what you've eaten for breakfast, lunch and dinner for the last five days, just by looking at your shirt.
>
> 2. When the 'Deodorant Fairy' pays you a visit.
>
> 3. When after you leave a washroom someone hangs a sign that says, "Toxic Area. Danger. Do Not Enter!"
>
> 4. When you're singing while you work, and the entire office gives you a standing ovation...when you stop!
>
> 5. You burp, and babies who can't even walk, run!

Language, Race and Humor

How many babies does it take to change a light bulb? The answer is: What's a light bulb? This joke hopefully didn't offend anyone reading this book. Probably not—because there are very few babies working in the average workplace. All the rest of us have things that we happen to be, such as a member of a cultural group, a religion, or gender. We may have different beliefs and morals from someone telling a joke, and that means that someone's joke might offend us.

Any joke involving a racial or religious group is not appropriate at work. It hurts people's feelings, offends them, making it difficult for members of that group to trust you and work side-by-side with you in the future. Likewise, jokes with strong sexual content or language that some might find offensive are also taboo. The rule is: If it could offend someone—don't say it.

"Did you hear about the Martian who put birdseed in his shoes to feed his pigeon toes?"

Another important area of courtesy is your language. For some people swearing comes naturally—it's a difficult habit to break. Try your very best! Swearing offends many people. The offended people could be coworkers who then find it hard to be around you, or it could be a customer your place of work may lose. You may feel it's your "right" to use any words you choose, but what about the "rights" of the person who has to hear them?

Being Courteous

When someone first learns the English language, the first five words they generally learn are: 1. *Hello* 2. *Good-bye* 3. *Please* 4. *Thank You* 5. *You're Welcome.* The reason these words are so important is they show we have courtesy, and people like to be treated with courtesy. Another great way to show courtesy is by complimenting someone. Find something nice to say about a customer or coworker and watch what happens! "Your hair looks nice," or "You're doing a great job," go a long way. When giving a compliment make it sincere. Avoid going overboard.

When a compliment goes overboard.

Letting Go Of the Past

Many of the problems we have in our relationships with others are because of what happened in the past. There are few things as powerful as forgiveness. Never mind who was right or who was wrong—it is far less important than you think it is. Treat every moment in your relationships as a new beginning and watch what happens.

"Remember the time in 1959?...You took my jelly doughnut!"

Compromise

Here's a common thing that happens in a workplace: people wanting different things. Has that ever happened in your workplace? The solution can be a power struggle, where one person or group wears the other down. Or maybe you have a thumb war—winner takes all! Or here's an even better solution: **find a compromise!** The way to get along, and for workplace peace, is compromise!

"We need to reach an agreement on the thermostat settings. The cold people have declared war on the hot people!"

Now let's examine an important part of workplace life, and happiness, that's easy for some, and more difficult for others...**Making friends at work.**

> *"You only meet your once in a lifetime friend—once in a lifetime." — from the 1940's TV Show, The Little Rascals*

Everything has to start somewhere. We all had a first day of school that began many years of school. We all have a first day on the job, which may be the beginning of many years with that workplace. And we'll all have strong and important new friendships in our lives that begin with that very first, **"Hello."**

What is a Friend?

There is no one way to define what a friend is. Being a friend might mean something very different to you than it does to me. Here are some of my thoughts: A friend is someone whose company you enjoy. A friend is someone who accepts you for who you are. A friend is there for you even when you mess up. A friend is someone who's genuinely excited for you when good things happen for you.

My advice is to look for **positive friends** who:

1.   Are enthusiastic about seeing you
2.   Push you to do your best and rise to challenges
3.   Support and encourage you
4.   Make you laugh and smile and feel good about yourself

As opposed to **negative friends** who:

1.   Constantly leave you depressed after you see them
2.   Make you feel angry or criticized
3.   Pour cold water on your dreams or ideas
4.   Make you feel lousy about yourself

Recipe for Making a Friend

The following is a very simple recipe for making friends. There are 6 ingredients. I'll demonstrate the recipe by making friends with you.

1. Smile and Show You're Friendly

Are you a sour person or a sunny one? Likeable people give loud signals of their desire to be friendly. They are warm and easygoing. It's as though they invite you to come in, like a restaurant with a sign that says, **"Open for Business."**

SO, HERE'S A PICTURE
OF ME. AS YOU CAN
SEE, I'M SMILING AND
FRIENDLY. SO, HOPE-
FULLY, IT'S THE FIRST
STEP TOWARD YOU
LIKING ME.

2. Like Them

We tend to like people who show that they like us. Liking someone is a compliment. When people think you like them, you become approachable instead of
distant. So the next step in the making a friend recipe is to show the other person
that you like them. So, I might say to you, **"You seem like a very interesting
person. I'd enjoy talking to you."**

3. Sincere Flattery

Find something you can make a sincere little compliment about, nothing over-
blown. Maybe it's something they're wearing, how they do their job, or about
their great sense of humor. I might say to you, **"I sure like your shirt. Where'd
you get it?"**

4. Point Out Similarities

Figure out what you have in common with that person. Maybe it's something as
simple as the fact you're both doing the same job or both wearing red. Similarities
are good conversation starters. I might say to you, **"I see we are both reading
the same book."**

5. Ask Questions

The best way to learn about someone is by asking questions. People usually enjoy
talking about themselves. You might want to ask them, "How long have you
worked here?" or "Where are you from?" or **"What do you like?"**

6. Create Feeling

When you meet someone for the first time it helps to create some feelings between you known as **empathy**. These feelings happen because most people are decent, and if they know you need something, they'll want to help you. For instance, you might tell someone that you're new and ask for help. Look for a shared interest to talk about, and be friendly

"Have you tried it with marinara sauce? Delicious!"

The importance of Smiling

How many languages can you speak? For most of us the answer is only one. So, how do you make friends with someone who doesn't speak much English or speaks another language than you do? People do it all the time, making friends without speaking. The key is something that is the same in all 252 languages in the world—**a smile!**

121

It takes 26 of our facial muscles to smile and 62 facial muscles to frown. So frowning is actually much harder to do than smiling. Try frowning and then smiling, and see which one feels like more work for your facial muscles.

Asking Questions

Asking questions is how we find out what we have in common with someone else, which is one of the most important ways of becoming friends. Asking questions to learn about a person serves two purposes. First, you learn more about what you might have in common. Second, asking questions means you're showing an interest. People respond with friendship when others show an interest in them. Some examples of questions to ask are:

1. Do you have a dog or cat?
2. Where are you originally from? What's it like there?
3. What do you like to do for fun or hobbies?
4. What kind of music do you like? What bands?

Feelers and Thinkers

Are there people you seem to just battle with all the time? Do you see white when they see black? There's a good chance the reason is that one of you is a **feeler** and the other one is a **thinker.**

Feelers focus on their feeling and how others behave towards them.
1. Constantly worried about what others feel about them
2. Will spend lots of time picking out the right card for someone
3. More sentimental, for instance, they like emotional movies
4. Like to discuss their feelings as a way to work things out
5. Very sensitive; often take things personally. They don't like conflict.

Thinkers don't like talking about or dealing with their feelings.
1. They are more aggressive and assertive, more likely for conflict
2. They like to get right to the point
3. They're more about facts than they are about emotions
4. They're inclined to pick out the first greeting card they see
5. Less sentimental; they like more action style movies

Thinkers and Feelers trying to co-exist in the animal world.

Women and Men: 65% of women are feelers and 35% are thinkers. In men, it's the opposite: 65% are thinkers and 35% are feelers. So, often the conflict is not between men and women at all, but rather between a feeler and a thinker. Are thinkers and feelers, masculine or feminine? Definitely not! For instance, take the movie Rocky. Rocky Balboa was sentimental, constantly dealing with his feelings, and spent a lot of effort planning out the most romantic dates and picking out gifts for Adrian— **a definite feeler!**

How Arguments Happen: If a **feeler** is asked **how they feel**, they will like that question, and give a detailed answer, telling you everything they are feeling. Ask a **thinker** how **they're feeling** and they'll get annoyed, and you'll usually wind up with an argument. Thinkers don't want to discuss their feelings.

A feeler gets upset when a thinker doesn't seem to care about their feelings, not realizing that it's a thinker's nature not to care about feelings. Thinkers don't ask feeling questions. They go straight to, "How do we solve this?"

Are you a thinker or a feeler? Make a list of people you know well, and decide if they're **thinkers** or **feelers**. Which group do you get along with best?

Dating Coworkers

It's tempting when you meet someone at work, and you hit it off. With each passing day, you talk back and forth, then you start dating each other. It seems like a good idea at the time—but then, not every romance ends like in a fairy tale, with Cinderella marrying her Prince. Most romances end up being more like Hansel and Gretel, where in the end somebody is always a witch.

Workplace romances are almost always a bad idea:

1. The relationship comes to an end. You may find this hard to believe, but not all breakups are good breakups. It may even have ended too badly for both of you to co-exist in the same workplace.

2. Dating can affect those around you while your romance is playing out in front of them. Many people will find your flirting back and forth distracting.

3. After breakups, co-workers are often forced to take sides. The breakup becomes a source of gossip, opinion and can create tension.

4. When you're in a workplace romance it's very hard for both of you to concentrate on doing your jobs.

© 2002 Randy Glasbergen.

"An office romance is so distracting.
I wasted the entire morning trying to fax you a hickey!"

McGivney, who had owned Bagpipes Are Us for 30 years, thought about it and realized nobody really knows the answer..."When is it time to tune a bagpipe?"

"Are you really listening —or are you just waiting for your turn to talk?"
—Robert Montgomery

127

Here's an interesting fact about the human body. Just about every one of us was born with two ears and only one mouth. Therefore we should do twice as much **listening as we do talking**. That being the case, this chapter on communicating is twice as much about the important **skill of listening** as it is about talking.

Is This You?

What does listening even mean? If you think that it's just about how much of the time you're speaking versus how much of the time the other person's speaking, you're wrong. Some people who say very little are still bad listeners. Listening is only partly about letting the other person talk. It's also about how well you pay attention to what the other person has to say.

Have you ever had this experience: Someone is talking to you about something, maybe a friend, a coworker, even a manager. But your thoughts have drifted, or you're so focused on what you're going to say next, you aren't sure at all what the other person even said. Most of us have had this experience—*constantly!*

Do You Listen?

It's a *good question* we should all ask ourselves. **Do we listen?** There's this idea floating about that it's men who're bad listeners. As a man, I don't know if men are any guiltier of not listening than women are. Some men are great listeners, and a lot of women are very poor listeners. The point for everyone is, how can you ask someone to listen to you, and really hear what you have to say, especially if it is something important to you, *if you don't listen?*

"It's a new invention of mine...I call it a Tearing Aid. If someone doesn't listen, then there's definitely going to be Tears."

The Benefits of Listening

As a good listener you'll enjoy better connections with people as listening builds stronger relationships. It makes you seem considerate, a nice person. Good listeners are viewed as alert and intelligent, competent and on top of things. Good listeners stay out of trouble! Bad listeners are constantly in hot water because not listening makes them miss something important and mess up. Getting our point across comes down to **listening**, not talking. When we listen, we **hear** where the other person is coming from. Then we know how to **respond** and **make our point**.

"The last thing Olga remembered is she was having a conversation with a co-worker, something about some work they were doing together... but as usual she wasn't paying much attention to anything her co-worker was saying...Then there might have been something mentioned about a fire."

How to Listen

Make good eye contact. Look directly in the eyes of the speaker. Eye contact tells the speaker you're paying attention. Without eye contact, the speaker will think you are not interested.

Avoid interrupting. Wait until the speaker is done before jumping in.

Stay focused. Don't wander with your eyes or mind.

Avoid yawning, or any other signs of boredom.

Give feedback. That could mean nodding your head to show you understand, or small comments like "Hummm," or "That's interesting".

Ask questions to show you're involved in what they are talking about, such as, "What did you do next?"

Did You Know? When babies are just two-days-old, they begin to recognize their mother's faces by looking at their mother's eyes. Even babies know the importance of eye contact.

So what's the opposite of a **Great Listener?** It's a **Motor Mouth**

You know you have a Motor Mouth Problem when...

1. The person you are talking to celebrates two birthdays before you finish your point.

2. You ask someone for a minute of their time and they pull out a calendar and start ripping out pages.

3. Instead of giving you pills to cure your laryngitis the doctor gives you pills to make it last longer.

4. Your country recruits you for the army, in the hopes you'll get captured, just to annoy the enemy.

5. You've been known to spend three hours on the phone explaining to the other person that it's a wrong number.

6. You're asked to bow your head for a minute of silence, but you can only make it 15 seconds.

Your Turn to Talk

Now that you've mastered being a great listener, it's **"Your Turn to speak!"**

How to Talk

Look at the person you are speaking to. Just like listening, talking, too, is about eye contact. When you look at somebody, it makes them far more interested in what you have to say.

Show emotion in your facial expressions.

Show emotions in your words. Talking is even more about your tone or emotions, than your words. Emotions such as enthusiasm can make even dull words more exciting.

Project with your voice, speak your words clearly, and don't mumble. Be careful to talk at the right speed, not too fast to where people miss words or so slow that people lose interest.

Model. Find someone you think is a good speaker and copy how they use their voice to communicate.

Share. Be careful you are not speaking too much, making long speeches or dominating the conversation. This will cause others to lose interest. **Don't be a motor mouth.**

Did You Know?

People talk at an average rate of 125 to 225 words a minute. 125 words is a slow talker, 225 a fast talker. **Which are you?**

© 2004 by Randy Glasbergen.
www.glasbergen.com

"This is the nicest conversation we've had in weeks.
Let's not spoil it by talking."

Timing

If someone is busy, it may not be the best time to interrupt them. Many people feel when they have anything at all on their mind to say, they can interrupt anybody, at any time, to say it! This kind of thinking is annoying to the person being interrupted, and it's rude. Worst of all are the constant interrupters. The people who have something to add to the last thing they had to say every few minutes. If this is a habit you have, learn to store matters you need to talk about and wait until the timing is better.

Another issue you need to consider is whether the place you are in is the appropriate place for a conversation. For instance, don't have a conversation that disturbs other people around you, who are trying to focus on their work.

Another consideration is privacy. Certain topics shouldn't be discussed in a public place where conversations can be overheard. This could be discussion about a coworker, or information about your job, best left private. Job complaints, for instance, should always be left to private conversations.

Copyright 2002 by Randy Glasbergen.
www.glasbergen.com

"I've seen the error of my ways and I've decided to start being more respectful to my coworkers. Hey, bozo, I'm talking to you!"

The Importance of Word Choices

There are actually three parts to communicating your thoughts to others, or what's called talking. First, the **words actually said**. Second, the way that you say the words, called your **tone of voice**. And third, your **body language**.

133

Neuro Linguistic Programming (NLP) is the science of selecting words that make you feel better about yourself. For instance, if someone asks you how you are feeling, you might answer, "Okay." What kind of message are you sending to your own brain? Okay is a bland word—it's hum-drum or so-so. Kind of like those hard candies that restaurants serve you after a meal—a so-so desert. Whereas answering "Great!" or "Fantastic!" to the same question is more like pie for desert! Makes you feel, well, *fantastic!*

Think of the words you use a lot. Are they positive words, making your feel good, or negative ones? For instance, someone asks how your job is going. Instead of saying, "All right" say, **"Super!"** and see how super you then feel. Instead of saying you're "frustrated" say you're **"challenged."** It'll make you feel better. Or instead of being angry be **"disappointed."**

THOMAS SMITH
DAN GIBSON

"Bob was a Neuro-linguistic motivational speaker...Don't think of him as dead, think of him as breathing challenged."

Try to choose words to make yourself and others feel better.

I Screwed up	I'm Learning
I'm Overwhelmed	I'm very Busy
I Failed	I Had a Temporary Setback
I've been Insulted	I've been Misunderstood
I'm feeling Good	I'm feeling Amazing
You Look Nice	You Look Sensational
That Person's Weird	That Person's Different

Tonality

The second part of talking is your tone of voice or **tonality**. It's often not the words you say that matter, but the way you say them. When Steve Martin began his comedy career on Saturday Night Live in the 1970s, one of his most famous routines was just saying three words: *"Well, ex-cuuuse me!"* It wasn't the words themselves, but how he said them, that made it so funny.

Think about saying to someone, "Get out of here." It can be said as an angry threat, or as a humorous reaction to what someone said they did. If you say, "You're crazy," it can be an insult, or a fun comment to a friend—depending on your tone of voice. You can say "Thank you", nicely or sarcastically. Or when asked to do something, if you say, "I'll do it," could mean you'll do it gladly, or that you'll do it, but you're unhappy about doing it.

Body Language

The third way we talk is with our body, which has a language all of its own, known as **body language**. Let's start with your face. When your eyes are wide and your eyebrows are raised, it means you're interested, pleased or excited. When your eyes become narrow, it means the opposite: You're bored, sad, angry, or upset.

Our arms are another body part we use to talk with. When we have our arms spread open it's called open body language. It means we're friendly and approachable. It sends messages of trust and warmth. People will want to be around us. When our arms are crossed, even clenched, that's closed body language, which says to people, "Stay away," or "I'm not friendly, so leave me alone." Be careful you're not sending, get lost signals, with your arms.

You know you Speak with Your Arms Too Much when...

1. You're making your point, the cat ends up flying across the room.
2. You say, "Oh my gosh!" and accidentally hit yourself so hard in the head, that you end up in a coma.
3. You have to call your insurance agent to report a damage claim following every interesting conversation you have
4. You put out the candles on your birthday cake without blowing.
5. When your career counselor in high school suggested you become an Air Traffic Controller.

Some sound advice. People who speak with their hands and arms should shower frequently and wear deodorant.

Tonality

Here's a body language technique for gaining confidence that will work every time, if you practice. It's your posture. Stand up straight, with your head held up high, your stomach tucked in, looking straight forward at the person you're talking to. That posture will immediately change the way people respond to you. People will treat you with respect and trust. ***Try it!***

Language Barriers

Here's what a person with another language does to understand:

1. Hears what you had to say, your words in English
2. Translates it into their language in their head
3. Decides how to answer you back in their language
4. Then translates it in their head before saying it in English

All this takes time. Help out, by speaking slowly and clearly. Use simple language and avoid slang they won't understand. Be patient! Give them time to understand and respond.

Full Day Exercise

This is an important one! Spend a day listening. Speak only when you need to. Focus on really listening. Hear what other people have to say and what they want. The key to this exercise is really paying attention.

"You are, without a doubt, the most disorganized person I've ever met!"

"Organization is what you do before you do something, so that when you do it, it's not all mixed up." — *A.A. Milne*

Excerpts from 'Dear Diary':

I can't take it anymore—today is the day that I'm going to get organized. I realize that I have said this before, for instance, January 1, New Year's Day, my resolution was to get more organized. But New Year's Day, I was tired from being out late. My place was a mess! It's very hard to get organized with all that confetti still in your hair. I had a few drinks the night before, but that didn't affect me. No, it was definitely the confetti. Everyone knows confetti dulls the mind. I had a few other New Year's resolutions, but somebody came over with pound cake, and there went that "Lose 20 pounds by February 1" resolution. Just like Christmas—on January 2, I checked my New Year's resolution list twice, and discovered—I'd been naughty, not nice.

January 12, that was the day I went grocery shopping, drove home and got a call from the grocery store that I had left my 2-year-old in the grocery cart, and he wanted to come home. Now that was embarrassing! So, I wrote you again, "Today's the day—from now on I'm going to be organized for the rest of my life. This time for sure!"

January 23, Today's the day, this time absolutely, positively for sure! I'm going to be organized from now on! I think that was the day I locked my keys in the car. It used to be so easy. You could open a car lock with a coat hanger. They just don't make car locks like they did in the good old days.

January 28, I'm sure I had my dog when I started the walk, but my brain got busy thinking, and then I got home, and strange as it was, there was no leash in my hand, and no dog. "Today's the day! For real!"

February and March I never wrote you, Dear Diary, not even once, about getting organized. Of course those were the two months I couldn't find my diary, so I didn't write you about anything.

April, I was to be too busy hanging out with my co-workers to worry about organization. April is tax refund month and that means money to spend. If I had only filed my return on time!

Today, this brings me to today. "This time today's really going to be it---the day I get organized!'" Today was the last straw. I was given the job of handing out 120 pay checks at the end of the day. But the Nut Guy came, the guy who goes around selling nuts and candy in my workplace, and after eating too many jujubes and Spanish peanuts, somewhere between the confusion of my trip to my car to find my wallet to pay for more jujubes, or my trip to the pop machine well, somehow, 120 pay checks got lost. The company says they can re-issue them all on Monday, but in the meantime, I'm not planning to hang out with anyone from work this weekend. So I have plenty of time, Dear Diary, to actually do it this time. **Get organized!**

Tonality

There's a common complaint just about all of us have—not enough time! Not enough time to get all of your work done, or time to get ready for work, not enough time for the other things needing to be done besides work. Just plain not enough time!

Time is the same for all of us. Each of us has 60 minutes in an hour, 7 days in a week and 52 weeks in a year—no more, no less. People often wish there were more hours in the day— though we can use our time wiser and gain more from our hours, there's still the same exact number of hours in everyone's day.

We can't change the amount of time we have, but we can change how well we use our time. How much time we use productively and how much time we waste. When you're working, you can get more done or less done, depending upon how you use time. When you're relaxing you can do things that are fun or spend the day doing nothing at all. It's said, "Life's short, there isn't enough time." Time is about valuing time. Ask yourself one vital question at the end of each day: Did I get the most out of my day?

Copyright 2002 by Randy Glasbergen.
www.glasbergen.com

GLASBERGEN

"You just spent 45 minutes explaining why you're too busy to do something that would have taken 2 minutes."

To be Productive — It Helps to Have a Plan

Most of us make the best use of our time at work when we have a plan. Without a plan we become easily lost, not knowing what to do next. For instance, picture yourself going on a holiday without a plan. With your suitcases packed, you realize you have no idea where you're even going

Not having a destination for a vacation, and just winging it, might be an interesting adventure once in a while. But how would you pack? Beach clothes or snow gear? To use our time in the wisest way, we're almost always most effective with a plan—knowing exactly where we're going and how we're going to get there.

A plan always involves knowing what it is you're looking to accomplish. If your job is to peel 10 potatoes, it doesn't matter how many oranges you squeeze, or how quickly you squeeze them, you're never going to get 10 potatoes peeled. To have the right plan, first be clear on what your tasks even are. If you need to clarify, then always ask. Then focus on your plan and don't get sidetracked by doing things that won't help you get it done.

Prioritizing

Has this ever happened to you? You find yourself with more than one task to do—of course, this happens to everyone! There's times when we can do more than one job at once—at other times, one task requires so much work that it's all that we can handle. How we handle multiple tasks is by prioritizing—picking the job that's most important or urgent first, then the next critical one after that, and so on. Many people have a bad tendency to pick the easiest job to do first. But when you avoid getting the most urgent job done, that just makes yours or someone else's job, harder later. If you don't know what the priorities should be, then ask.

"Thanks, boss, I'm glad you cleared that up. So adding up the number of paper clips in my drawer isn't my highest priority then."

Crisis Management

Here's another way people often decide on their priorities—by crisis! A task only makes it to the top of their list when it becomes an emergency—when if they don't do it this very second, then it'll come crashing down on them! If they don't deal with this piece of equipment right away, it'll blow up! If they don't have their paperwork in right now, the boss will blow a gasket! Their car is on fire, so it might be time to change the oil! The problem with crisis management is problems are harder to handle once they're a crisis.

In retrospect, Mike wondered whether it might have been a good idea to cut the grass three months ago.

Being Efficient in Your Job

There are times when we need to speed up. When the work is piled up, going faster is a necessity. A restaurant in the heat of lunch rush couldn't get everyone served without speeding up. Like a car, sometimes we need to hit our gas pedal a bit harder, too. Most of us can speed up most tasks when we want to—we just have to want to! Want proof? Tell a teenager she can't go out until her room's clean, then watch her speed up—to get that job done.

Perfectionism — Slows You Down

Some people are perfectionists—they keep working on a task until it's flawless, doing it over and over until they're satisfied with the results. And that's great, because there are times when being perfect is important. Take brain surgery. Most of us would like to have a surgeon working on our brain who was a perfectionist, not a surgeon who took 30 seconds, then said, "Good enough."

Most of the tasks we do aren't surgery. The problem with being a perfectionist is most jobs require you to get lots of work done—getting things perfect stands in the way of maximum productivity. If you're a perfectionist, ask a manager to help you judge when a job's done well enough and it's time to push on.

I did it! I finally did it! It took me 15 attempts, and the entire day to accomplish it, but I did it...the perfect grilled cheese sandwich.

Doing Your Job Too Quickly

It's a problem being too perfect—but, when you do things too quickly, it can lead to mistakes. Making a mistake often puts you back to square one, and actually lose time doing something over. Go fast or go slow—what to do? Picture yourself as a wedding cake baker. Which one's you? Hopefully neither.

A difference in cake attitude.

Think of this **balance** as a glass on a table. If you're being careful but doing things too slowly, then your pace becomes a problem—everyone suffers because you're not getting enough work done. If you're fast, but making lots of mistakes, then that's a different problem—everyone suffers from your carelessness. You need to be the third table, the one with the glass in the middle, doing things fast enough, but with care. That's **balance!**

| Doing things too slowly and carefully | Doing things too fast and carelessly | The perfect balance! |

Organization

It's in our worst moments of disorganization, that we tend to hate ourselves the most. Who can like themselves after three hour of looking for keys or a wallet? Or when you have to call a towing truck because you locked your keys in your car? According to an Accountemps survey, the amount of time the average person looks for lost things adds up to 5 weeks out of every year! **Isn't there something else you'd rather do with 5 weeks?**

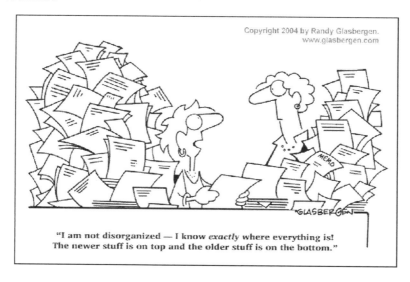

Copyright 2004 by Randy Glasbergen.
www.glasbergen.com

"I am not disorganized — I know *exactly* where everything is! The newer stuff is on top and the older stuff is on the bottom."

You know you Have an Organization Problem when...

1. People kept telling you that you needed to buy a watch, so you bought a watch—but now you can't find it.
2. You lock your keys in the car, but you have no way to pay for a tow truck, because you can't find your wallet.
3. A group of people at work go in on a lottery ticket, and win 20 million dollars—but you've lost the ticket.
4. You finally arrive for a lunch meeting and the moon is out.

How to be Organized

Being organized saves a great deal of time and makes us more productive. Organization reduces our stress. We get into less trouble with others, because being organized, we make far fewer mistakes. Organized people are more successful at everything—than disorganized people. Most important, feeling organized makes people feel happy! No one feels good about themselves when they're in chaos. **There are two keys to being organized:**

Key One: Your Habits. Organization is about your habits. If you have clutter around you, or don't put things away, that's a bad habit. Make a good habit of keeping your work area uncluttered and well organized. For instance, put work items, or keys, in the same place each time.

"According to FAA statistics, each year a surprising number of flight delays are caused by pilots who can't find their keys."

Key Two: Writing Things Down. We all have important thoughts and ideas which we make the mistake of keeping just in our heads. Then later we can't remember what these thoughts even were. Nothing is more frustrating! Writing things on bits of paper or napkins is almost as bad as not writing things down at all. Get into the habit of carrying a Day-Timer or a notebook with you. Make notes, and lists of items you need to get, and lists of things needing to get done.

Life Tip

Daily Task Lists or To-Do Lists are great ways to stay organized. Get into the habit of taking a few minutes, either before you go to bed at night or first thing in the morning, to make a list of things you need to do that day, using your notebook. The few minutes it takes to make the list will save you hours of time!

Great Workplace Moments: Simon comes up with an ingenious way to remind himself not to forget important things...Of course a notebook would have worked even better, and at a fraction of the cost!

Full Day Exercise

What is your biggest single problem at work? Not using time as well as you could? or being disorganized? If it's a time use problem, then take a full day to really focus on not wasting time and using time as effectively as you can. If it's disorganization, spend the day focusing on really being organized, including using a notebook, making a to-do list, and cleaning up clutter. If it's both, then take two days, one day for each!

"The low-carb people demanded it."

"The nicest thing about teamwork is that you always have someone on your side." —*Margaret Carty*

> *"None of us are as smart as all of us."* —Japanese Proverb

The Opposite of Teamwork — Being a Hermit

A hermit is a person who lives alone, usually in a cave. Hermits almost never see other people. Most of us, some of the time, would probably envy the life of a hermit. There are times when we think, "Wouldn't it be great if everyone just left us alone."

Being part of a team, such as a workplace, has its challenges and frustrations. But when a group of people pull together, each helping in their own way, it's amazing what can be accomplished and how great it can feel to be part of that **team experience.**

Tragically, Frank learned the hard way that one person should never try and enter a parade all by himself, as a marching band.

The world's record for one man running a 400-meter race is 43 seconds. The world's record for the 400-meter relay, where the same distance is run by four runners sharing the run—drops down to 38 seconds. That's a much faster time, *because of teamwork.*

> I love to hear a choir. I love the humanity, to see the faces of real people devoting themselves to a piece of music. I like the TEAMWORK. It makes me feel optimistic about the human race when I see them cooperating like that.
> **—Paul McCartney, the Beatles**

The examples of the importance of teamwork are numerous. Even the greatest athletes wouldn't stand a chance against another team just by themselves. Imagine being the only player on a hockey team: You'd be forward, then goalie, then back to forward. It could get tiring. Or moving a piano—it doesn't matter how strong you are, you just can't move a piano alone. You may as well have no muscles at all, because that piano is going nowhere. But iwith 3 helpers, now that piano will get somewhere.

Everyone on the Team is Valuable

Sadly, we live in a society that tends to put the greatest value on who are famous. If we happen to be in a restaurant and Hal the plumber is sitting with Meg in accounting, chances are we wouldn't take notice. But if we came in the restaurant, and Brad Pitt was sitting with Julia Roberts, our eyes would bug out of our heads. And then if Brad or Julia leaned over and asked if they to borrow our salt, after leaving the restaurant we'd call everyone we know, "Guess who borrowed my salt!" But if Hal the plumber asked to borrow our salt, some of us wouldn't even pass the salt. We certainly wouldn't call a friend to say, "Guess what, a plumber borrowed my salt!" But when 200 people need to get paid, it's Sandy in accounting that comes through, not Julia Roberts—and if you ever have an overflowing toilet, I doubt if you can get Brad Pitt to take a look.

Copyright 2002 by Randy Glasbergen.
www.glasbergen.com

"You were my imaginary friend, we had some great times. But I haven't heard from you since I was five years old and now you show up and expect me to give you a job?"

Everyone's a Team Member

There are two rules to being on a team:

Rule One: You're as important as anyone else on the team.

Rule Two: Everyone else on the team is as vital as you.

It's the same in any workplace. In a workplace **a team is**, people pulling together with a common cause, getting a job done.

There is an old fable about a house and an argument that takes place between the parts of the house about which part is most important. The foundation says it is most important, because the rest of the house rests on top of it, and without it the house would collapse. The walls say that they are the most important because without walls there can't be a house. The floor then speaks up and says it is the most important, because without a floor to walk on there's no point to having a foundation or walls. Then the windows make their claim: Who would want to live in a house without windows? The door suggests that without doors there'd be no way to get in. Finally the roof makes a good point—it's the most important, because without a roof people in the house would get rained on and snowed on, and have a pretty miserable time. When all of the parts of the house took the time to hear each other's point of view they realized that none of them could function and form a house without all of them. Therefore, the parts of the house concluded that: **All of them were the most important.**

After learning the value of Teamwork, Bowser and Rex became legends at chasing cars...Eventually they were able to open their own car lot.

There Are All Types of People On Your Team

Meet Sarah, she's 41, she's a manager. Sarah is also the mother of three children—Sarah's on the team. Meet Tran, he's 30, he's a computer specialist who moved from Vietnam when he was a child—Tran's on the team. Meet Peter, who's 62. He has a champion collie and goes to dog shows all over the country. He's in maintenance—Peter's on the team. Meet Jennifer, she's 19, she just started in customer service, and she wants to go back to school and become an actress—Jennifer's on the team. Meet Jan, she's 50. She's been the boss for 12 years. She's going to retire in 5 years then go to Africa to help build villages—Jan's on the team.

We're All Different: Which Makes Teams Great

Members of a team do all kinds of different jobs—some wear business suits and some wear jeans and a T-shirt or a uniform. Some people have been with the company for years. Others started their job only a short time ago. Some speak English as their language—some speak a different language.

One of the most significant differences between people on a team is age and experience. There are 4 groups that share a workplace:

Veterans: People over 59   **Boomers:** People 41 to 59
Generation Xers: People 25 to 40   **Generation Nexters:** People under 25

   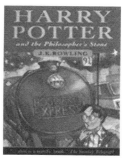

These groups can often look at one another with distrust and a lack of understanding, believing they have nothing in common. In truth they have lots to offer one another. When they pull together as a team, the team is stronger because of the different age groups. Each age group has its own unique talents that it brings to the team. *Boomers* and *Veterans* are strong on experience and have much to teach younger groups. *X'ers* and *Nexters* are full of fresh ideas, and are often skilled with technology they can share with the older groups.

Exercise Get to know as much about as many coworkers as you can. Learn more about their interests when they're not working. Get to know at least two people who work with you.

Making Your Team the Best

There are three things that go together to make a team the best team it can be: a **common goal**, **commitment** to the goal, and supporting each other through **cooperation**. Let's take a look at each of these things.

A Common Goal

The **best teams** are always the teams with the **best common goals**. In sports, the team that plays the best together usually wins, even when they have less talent then a team without great teamwork. No workplace can excel, unless the goals of the workplace are supported by each member of the team. So, ***put your team 1st!***

"Bob and Ed went into business together. Bob wanted to sell burgers. Ed wanted to sell milk. They do not have a common goal. Ultimately the business failed."

Commitment

The **best teams** are always the teams with committed team members, taking pride in their workplace's success. How well would a basketball team play if some of its players had an attitude that it really didn't matter to them whether the team won or not? In a workplace, the attitude of people who work there, positive or negative, including your attitude, spreads to others.

"I think Smith is showing a definite lack of commitment to the team".

Commitment

The **best teams** are always the teams whose members cooperate with one another. They also take it one step further by looking for ways **to help one another out**. When you help someone out, then when it's your turn to need help, someone will be there to help you, too.

"How can you say we're not behaving like a team?
We're all wearing the same color shirts, aren't we?"

Use these pages for your exercises or notes

Copyright 2002 by Randy Glasbergen.
www.glasbergen.com

GLASBERGEN

"Welcome to the Ego Repair Hotline!
Press 1 for 'Hey, you look great today!'
Press 2 for 'How did you get to be so smart?'
Press 3 for 'I wish I was more like you!'"

"Mr. Meant-to has a friend, his name is Didn't-Do. Have you met them? They live together in a house called Never-Win. And I am told that it is haunted by the Ghost of Might-have-Been." —*Marva Collins*

> "If you can't make a mistake, then you can't make anything." —Marva Collins

Mistakes: We've All Made Them

Whoever is reading this book and has never made a mistake, raise your hand—or, better yet, light your hair on fire! It's safe for me to write, "Light your hair on fire!", because I am certain everyone reading this book has made a mistake. Besides which, even if you actually have never made a mistake in your life, and you did light your hair on fire, well, that certainly qualifies as a mistake!

Every single person—corporate leaders, athletes and kings alike—make mistakes and have failed at things. Even Tiger Woods misses the cut once in a while. Okay, once in 137 golf tournaments, but once in a while.

One of my favorite mistake stories happened during an NFL football game. Jim Marshall, a tackle for the Minnesota Vikings picked up a fumble during the game and started running for the end zone to score a touchdown. It's a real rarity in football for a defensive tackle to score a touchdown—it might happen once every ten years or so. As Jim Marshall was running to score his famous touchdown, his teammates were screaming at him. It turns out he ran 70 yards in the wrong direction and didn't score a touchdown for his team. He scored against them! He also earned himself the nickname of 'Wrong Way Marshall.'

Some famous mistakes have even had happy endings. In 1886 a pharmacist named John Pemberton tried to create a medicine tonic for people who were tired, nervous, or had sore teeth. It didn't cure any of these things, but Pemberton liked the taste, so he began marketing it as a drink. And Coca-Cola was born! In the first year it was a flop, he sold only $50 worth of Coke. Eventually Coke succeeded, of course. Today, the world drinks Coke around 1 billion times a day. I take this as quite a story of encouragement for us every day screw-ups—to keep trying.

> *"More people would be learning more from their mistakes if they weren't so busy denying them."* — Harold Smith

HAPPY BIRTHDAY

"Fortunately the office had a very good Workman's Compensation Plan that covered cake."

Learning From Your Mistakes

Here's an important question to consider: How can you learn from your mistakes, if you never admit to actually making one?

Most people have a very false idea about mistakes. They have come to believe that the best strategy to follow is to rarely, if ever, admit their mistakes. They believe that if you make mistakes you must be weak or stupid! So if you never admit to a mistake, then you are never weak or stupid. Another false belief is that admitting to a mistake will always lead to getting into **more trouble.**

When mistakes happen, in most cases, other people like managers or supervisors have a pretty good idea of who made the mistake anyway. Facing your mistake and admitting to it is almost always the best strategy. Consider this: When we don't admit to our mistakes or failures we lose out on all there is to learn.

Life Tip

When you make a mistake, fess up and t**ake ownership of it.** People will respect you more and you'll respect yourself.

164

What We Learn From Our Mistakes

1. We learn to try harder and look for other answers, instead of just continuing on in the same way that caused the mistake in the first place.

2. We learn not to give up or quit, which is persistence.

3. We learn we can make a mistake or fail at something and survive. Making mistakes is rarely the end of the world.

Accepting our Mistakes...'But'

Besides people who can never admit to a mistake, is another group that is nearly as bad: the **Buts**. A **But** is a person who can admit to a mistake, but there's always a but following right after. **Buts** always give excuses like, "I did it, but it wasn't really my fault." A **But** has a reason for every mistake.

Not admitting to mistakes, or making excuses, causes people to lose respect for you. So, when you make a mistake, as we all do, admit to it, explaining if it helps, but don't make any excuse for your mistake. Apologize sincerely to anyone affected by your mistake. Then look for ways to fix the mistake or improve the situation.

THOMAS SMITH
DAN GIBSON

"OK, I'm dog enough to admit it...Not only did I drink from the toilet, but I'm the one who left the toilet seat up too."

A Riddle For You

Name a word that contains all of the first six letters in the English language: **a-b-c-d-e-f.** Here's your clue: It's a very positive word—something that will help you succeed in your job.'

Give up? The answer to the riddle is the word, **Feedback.**

In the workplace, the main way we learn to correct our mistakes and do our job better is through feedback. Feedback can come from our coworkers, who have been there longer, or who have developed a skill in a particular area where you might be lacking. Most often, feedback comes from a manager, supervisor or a boss.

Feedback from Managers

Providing feedback is a large part of a manager's job. Your manager is usually far more aware of what the workplace's needs and intentions are. Your manager is also aware of the plan that's in place to meet those intentions. Your manager knows how you and your job fit into what your workplace is trying to achieve. You may not be entirely aware of any of those things. What you assume your workplace's intentions are may not be correct.

So, the purpose of **feedback** is a **Good Purpose**. It's to help you do your job better for everyone's sake.

Copyright 2001 by Randy Glasbergen.
www.glasbergen.com

"It's a special hearing aid. It filters out criticism and amplifies compliments."

Feedback Isn't Criticism

Nobody likes to feel criticized. When someone is critical of us, most of us go on the defensive. Our instinct is to defend ourselves. What is at stake is our self-esteem and how we feel about ourselves. And it certainly isn't fun when someone says something that lowers our self-esteem.

How to Deal With a Manager Giving Your Feedback

1. Control your negative thoughts towards being criticized. Take it as feedback intended to help you succeed in your job.

2. Look for the truth in what you are being told.

3. Don't get angry or argue; listen carefully to the comments.

4. Ask for details on anything you don't understand. If your told they don't like the way you do something, ask what it is about the way you're doing it that they don't like, so you can walk away understanding—knowing what needs to be improved.

5. If the feedback has some truth to it, apologize, without making excuses, and let them know that you will sincerely try to correct what needs to be changed.

6. Don't let it affect your mood, or the rest of your day. Take it as an opportunity to improve and grow.

7. ***Then bounce back and try your best in the future.***

Criticism is any comment where a person intends to hurt or insult with words, especially when nothing useful can be served or learned. Whereas the intention of criticism is to be destructive, **feedback** is information or observations that someone gives you because they want to help you find a positive result, teach you, or help you do something better.

"You paid 8 Mountain Goat skins!...30 Years ago your mother and I bought our first cave for 3 Mountain Goat skins."

Giving Feedback

Always give feedback constructively, avoiding name-calling, or saying things that can damage someone's self-esteem. Figure out the specific thing that you want to accomplish, and try to keep it to *1 specific item*. People do not respond well to being hit with 100 different things at once—or *everything* that is the matter with them.

Surprisingly, Wilma and Al never became friends.

Timing of Feedback

There is one other huge mistake people often make when giving feedback, whether it's at work or with family or friends—it's picking the right timing. A lot of times feedback is given right after something happens, when people are still angry. When you give feedback when you're agitated or angry, or the person you're giving feedback to is angry, then that's the wrong timing. You'll end up with resistance, and maybe even a fight. And you definitely won't be able to provide constructive feedback.

Try this experiment. Stand up and hold out the palms of your hands so they are facing someone in front of you. Ask the person to put their palms to yours so they are touching. Now push their palms with your palms. The moment you push, the other person will react and push back. When you're angry or agitated and you pick that time to give someone feedback as to why you are angry—the same thing happens. You push, and the other person gets defensive, and pushes back. So, wait until a little time has passed, and you're less emotional as a better time to give feedback.

"It's worked wonders around here. There are hardly any complainers, gossipers, busybodies, malcontents, angry people or people who don't pull their own weight, left".

"The best way to knock a chip off someone's shoulder — is to slap them on the back." —Source Unknown

Dear Kevin:

I wanted to write this letter to tell you something important. I'm very sad that I will not be able to tell you to your face. Even though we only met for a few minutes, you changed my life and the way I will treat other people, forever.

We worked in the same place for the last 3 months, but I never talked to you. I remember when I first came to work I saw you around a couple of times and I asked someone who you were, and they just said, "Stay away." So I asked why and they said, "That kid's always in trouble, acting up, cussing people out, and steals things, too." So in the time we worked together I never said hello to you, never talked to you even once, I just stayed away. One time when $25 was missing from my purse, somebody said it was you who took it, but I never asked you about it. I just decided that they must have been right.

Then last Friday at the end of the day I saw you sitting in the parking lot after work and I thought you were crying. Something inside me made me go over to you, and you were upset. I asked you what was wrong and you told me you were just fired. I told you not to worry, you'd get another job, but you told me, "What's the difference? It's been the same everywhere." I asked you if you had family you could talk to, but you shook your head. That's when you let it all pour out of you. How your parents had been killed in a plane crash when you were eight, then how the next day you went to live with your aunt, but your uncle used to get drunk and beat you up. Your aunt didn't do anything about it, and your uncle would just laugh when he saw your bruises and tell you to stop crying and toughen up. I'll never forget asking you, "Isn't there a friend you can talk to?" You told me, "I don't remember ever having a friend." Then we said good-bye because my ride was there, and I told you to have a nice weekend. You told me, "You, too."

On Monday when I got to work, they were all talking about the accident, how you had gotten hit by a train and killed. The newspaper said you were drunk at the time. They also said you were 21 years old. I never knew your age, but you looked a lot older. That's the same age as me. People said you were a jerk, and they weren't very sad. I was sad. I had to leave work for a while because I was crying. I wondered if things would have turned out differently, had I only talked to you before last Friday. Maybe all you really needed was somebody to understand you. Somebody to be a friend.

Your Friend,

Katherine

Sometimes There's a Reason

When people behave in a way that impacts us, often what we notice is the behavior and not the person. We rarely ask about what the reasons for the behavior may be. Every parent knows that when a child exhibits bad behavior, it's usually because the child is crying out for attention. Children need attention. If they don't get positive attention, then they want **negative attention**, because that's at least better than no attention at all.

Here's a question: At what age do we stop needing attention? At what age is it that when we don't get attention, we no longer feel the need for negative attention? Does this end on your 8th birthday? Or perhaps the need for attention never really ends. Maybe, even when we're 90, we'll still crave attention. Elderly people, like everyone else, are still craving attention. It's not uncommon for a senior to resort to negative behavior to get it.

In this section we'll examine a lot of different behaviors you'll see in any workplace, and how to deal with them. The types of behavior we'll look at range from mildly irritating to outright angry and threatening. There are certain behaviors that shouldn't be tolerated, to be sure. But the one common thread in dealing with any behavior are these very, very important words, *being understanding*. That doesn't mean that you should accept someone's negative behavior—but you should try to be understanding of the person who behaves that way. Every behavior has a real person with real feelings, and real pain—behind it. Maybe if you know the real story, you can help.

Copyright 2003 by Randy Glasbergen.
www.glasbergen.com

"From now on, all job applicants must perform a musical number. We have too many tone-deaf people singing along to the radio!"

In a Workplace You Deal With Many Behaviors

There's a reason why Baskin-Robbins has 31 flavors—because we're all different and there's no one flavor that everyone likes. Different people have different strengths: Some of us can sing, and others of us would irritate the hearing impaired with our serenade. Some of us can dance. Others can paint. We're also different in the ways that we annoy others. None of us are immune. We all do something that gets on at least someone's nerves.

Not only do we get on the nerves of others, but there are things that others do that we don't always like. Sometimes we feel like taking one of our coworkers and swinging him or her through the air by the tie. If he or she isn't wearing a tie, then it would be worth it to buy them one, and then swing them through the air by it! However, tie-swinging is never the best answer. This chapter shows other strategies— that you can try instead.

Something else to remember. All of us are capable of change for the better. So, if you recognize yourself in any of the behaviors that irritate others and impact a workplace, then you, too, are capable of change. If you recognize that others have any of these behaviors, we'll discuss some strategies that might help. Here are some difficult people common to all workplaces:

Badgers: It doesn't matter what you are doing, whatever is on a badger's mind is more important. They always interrupt, badger you, and keep you from doing your job.

Copyright 1998 by Randy Glasbergen.

"I don't see how anybody can get any work done around here with all the noise. How can anyone concentrate with people jabbering all day? You'd think people would shut up so others could work. That's the thing that really bugs me, all the unnecessary chatter. People should be more considerate...."

Bashers: They have an opinion about everything you do and it's usually negative. Bashers love to put you down by shouting or being abusive.

Copyright 2002 by Randy Glasbergen.
www.glasbergen.com

"I'd like to learn how to be less critical. My mouth has been classified as a weapon of mass destruction."

Cover-Ups: They have an excuse for everything and can never be counted on. They're often late or missing, or don't get their work done. But it's never their fault.

© 1998 Randy Glasbergen.

"I'm going to be late for work this morning. I was listening to my motivation tapes and suddenly found myself driving farther and faster than I ever imagined I could!"

Boors: They are rude and inconsiderate to the needs of others. It doesn't matter to a boor that somebody else has a job to do. All that matters is their own needs.

It's also important to let the other guy finish his job.

Exploiters: They take advantage of you whenever they can. An exploiter is always looking for a way to find an edge for themselves at someone else's expense.

"Seeing as how you don't need it at the moment, I'm borrowing your car."

Procrastinator: They are people who rarely get around to what they say they are going to do, or what's asked of them. Procrastinators frustrate others trying to do their jobs.

In a time honored tradition going back to the pyramids, no construction worker has ever made a mistake that was actually their fault.

Buck Passers: They do not want to take any responsibility for anything. Whether it's a task they're supposed to do, or a mistake they've made, they pass responsibility elsewhere.

Lou, the Funeral Director, kept putting things off until the work really started to pile up.

Ego Trippers: They are arrogant, full of themselves and their own self-importance. Ego Trippers grab credit they don't deserve, and they often need to minimize everyone else.

"And now for my part...sharing credit for all the work."

Loafers: Their goal is to try to avoid work as much as possible. They prefer to do the bare minimum and leave the rest for someone else. Loafers are lazy with low energy.

"The reason I am late...The truth is I didn't want to leave my bed."

> *"Always forgive your enemies, nothing annoys them more."* —Oscar Wilde

The Part We Play

None of us have the power to change someone else. The only person that we have full control over is our own self. So, can we wave our magic wand and make someone else's behavior change? It would be nice, but of course we can't. We can, however, control our own reactions, and keep our cool, instead of being sucked into someone else's actions and moods. When we keep our cool, we almost always get better results.

Above all, we need to be conscious of our own moods and how they may contribute to the situation. When we are in a bad mood, or feel frustration, then something someone else does, something that wouldn't have mattered on another day—is suddenly getting under our skin and causing us to react. Be careful of your own moods. It's not just others that affect you with their moods, but **you affect others with your mood as well.**

"Your cologne smells like spice. Oregano is a spice. Pizza is made with oregano. Some people like pizza with pepperoni. Pepperoni is made from pigs. As a vegetarian, that offends me. I'm filing a complaint against you!"

Life Tip

Pick your battles very carefully and don't make everything a battle. Learn to walk away from a potential argument.

When Behavior Crosses the Line... *To Anger*

When someone becomes overly angry, they're almost always going too far. There are two types of anger: **spontaneous**, when a person flies off the handle without thinking, and **intentional**, when someone uses anger as a plan to scare others into getting their way. Sometimes when people get angry, they attempt to defend it by saying, "I was only trying to help," or "I was trying to get things resolved." There are **two types of reactions** to any situation: **constructive**, which is a solution that makes the situation better for everyone, and **destructive**, which may solve the problem for now, but makes the situation worse in the long run. Using anger as a tactic is almost always a destructive solution.

Anger happens when someone is **out of control** of their emotional state. When someone is in a state of anger, they do not think as well, work as well, or cooperate as well. Anger affects your heart, making it beat faster. Heart attacks are very common when people get too angry. Anger affects your digestive system, making your stomach hurt. It affects your immune system that keeps you from getting sick. People who get angry a lot are far more likely to get ill, getting everything from colds to cancer. Tumors are often linked to anger. Anger may well be as unhealthy or bad for you as smoking is. Anger includes several different behaviors: Angry Remarks, An Angry Voice, Attacks of Any Kind, Severe Criticism, Hurtful Sarcasm, Extreme or Loud Complaining, Violence.

How to Deal With Someone's Anger

The worst possible way to deal with someone else's anger is to get angry yourself. That is like adding flames to a fire. When two people are angry, the potential is ripe for the situation to turn ugly. The best strategy is to say to the angry person, "I don't care for your tone, and "I'll leave if you don't calm down." If the angry person doesn't calm down, *the solution is to leave.*

Dealing with an Angry Person

1. When people get angry, their body chemistry changes. Therefore, deal with their physical symptoms in order to get them to calm down. If they are pacing or standing, getting them to sit down will help a great deal.

2. Anger makes someone thirsty, so offer water, but never caffeine, such as coffee, which makes symptoms worse.

3. Hear them out. Let them know you're listening. Don't interrupt.

4. Stay calm. Never throw fuel on the fire. Leave if you need to. Always protect your own safety.

5. When in doubt, bring someone else in, such as a manager.

How to Deal With An Angry Customer

Often times when a customer is angry, it's because they don't feel that their needs are being met and they're frustrated. It may have nothing to do with you. Maybe that person has been in a long line, or on hold, and you're the first one to whom they can express their frustration. Show understanding. Listen carefully. Nod or give feedback to show you sympathize. First, deal with their feelings and then the problem. Ask what they'd like you to do to help. If you can't meet their need, offer what you can. At least you've shown you care. If the problem is too difficult, get a supervisor. Never allow yourself to take abuse. If the customer crosses that line, call for a manager to assist you.

Bullying and Abuse

Two extreme forms of anger that should never take place are **bullying** and **abuse**. These take place when somebody's anger becomes threatening to you. **You are always allowed to refuse abuse**. Under no circumstances should somebody else be allowed to frighten you, threaten you, intimidate you or torment you, even if you aren't doing your job properly.

However, you do need to recognize the difference between light teasing, that almost everyone gets, and abuse. Anything that is abuse needs to be reported at once to a supervisor or someone in Human Resources in a position to help. Bullying or abuse is any of the following:

1. Belittling or putting you down in a strong way, especially around others.
2. Shouting at you or threatening you in any way.
3. Making snide comments or comments meant to anger you.
4. Harsh criticism with a sarcastic tone.
5. Name calling in a hurtful way.
6. Any remark that is sexist, racist or refers to a disability.

Copyright 2004 by Randy Glasbergen.
www.glasbergen.com

"Yes, I think I have good people skills.
What kind of idiot question is that?"

Violence or Physical Threat

Violence or physical threatening is not only totally out of bounds in any workplace but also a criminal matter. If you have been the victim of violence, or have the fear that violence could take place, it needs to be **reported at once** to a supervisor or to security.

Sexual Harassment

Sexual harassment is usually thought of as a problem for women, but men can have the problem as well. If you're the victim, first off, it's nothing to be embarrassed or secretive about. Sexual harassment is a common problem more than 50% of women report they've experienced one or more times.

Sexual harassment is any behavior that's uncomfortable or unwelcome, including jokes and remarks, sexual teasing, taunts, body comments, displays of pornography or offensive pictures, practical jokes causing sexual embarrassment, unwelcome invitations or requests, gawking or suggestive gestures, sexist remarks about women in general, or unwelcome contact such as patting, touching, pinching, or physical assault of any kind.

If You're a Victim of Sexual Harassment

1. Tell the person you object to their behavior. Mean it!

2. Keep a written record of dates, times and details.

3. If it continues, report it to the appropriate person. If it still continues, government agencies exist in most cities where you can request help.

4. Most importantly, under no circumstances do you need to, or should you, tolerate any sexual harassment.

Personal Boundaries

Boundaries are **reasonable** lines we create, which others should respect. At work, you're entitled to your reasonable boundaries. You shouldn't have to tolerate rudeness, being around dangerous or illegal behavior, or violence or harassment of any kind. If somebody puts you down, makes you feel as though you have no value—or treats you in any abusive manner, i**t's time to act**. Change this! Set those reasonable personal boundaries others are not allowed to cross without an invitation. The key word is **reasonable**. Avoid being overly sensitive with your boundaries.

© 1998 Randy Glasbergen.
www.glasbergen.

"I believe it's important to be sensitive to the needs of our employees...but do we really need a paper cut support group?"

Don't React to Anger...By Getting Angry Too

The *other guy* is often trying to goad us into a fight or get us upset. It's his or her aim to try and make you feel awful! Anger drags us down, even when the angry episode is over. Chances are it'll ruin your day, maybe your entire week.

Sometimes we can't help getting angry, because it just happens. If you're angry: Do deep breathing, take slow deep breaths. Drink water. Leave the situation and go for a timeout—or consult a friend, telling them you want to be calmed down. Think seriously about what you have to gain from the situation by being angry. Or what you might lose!

If you are somebody who either solves problems or often deals with a situation by getting angry, then think again! You've heard it said 1,000 times before, and it's true: **Anger Solves Nothing!'**

It happens all the time just like that...**yah right!**

Resolving the Conflict...**Nicely!**

The first ingredient in solving any argument nicely is fairness. Both people in a dispute need to be fair to each other. Fairness comes from seeing each other's point of view. But—what if the other person doesn't see yours? Then guess what? You get an honor. You get to be the **bigger person**. You get to accomplish this by seeing their point of view, first. When you do so, and in a nice way, this will then help them see your point of view. Hopefully, this can be the first step leading to a compromise.

Compromise...Known as a **Win-Win** Solution

People often confuse **win-win** with, **"I Win."** Win-win solutions happen when a compromise is found where everyone gets part of what they want. "This time you pick, next time I do," is a win-win, or "You do this part of the task," and "I'll do that part."

"How about this for a win-win situation? You buy this house now, and when you're miserable living there...I'll sell you another one. That way it's a win-win situation...For Me!"

The **Agree to Disagree** Solution

Not all arguments can be won. Why? Because we don't think the very same way. At times we have to acknowledge a particular disagreement has no resolution. We can walk away frustrated—or—**we can agree to disagree.**

"It's my opinion I should eat you. I take it that it's your opinion I should let you go. Why don't we just Agree to Disagree."

"Experts say that petting a cat is a good way to reduce stress...but nobody told the cat!"

"You have to take the bitter with the sweet."
—Samuel Goldwyn

What More can Possible Happen to Me?

Do you ever ask this question, **"Why me?"** Does it ever feel as though you have more than your weight of problems on your shoulders? In fact, are there times when you feel you have enough problems for 6 people's shoulders?

It happens to almost all of us—those times when life feels like a blizzard, pounding us with snow. When, as though we don't have enough problems, or enough to feel depressed about, we're handed even more problems. ***It just doesn't seem fair!***

But the **Good News** is...

Every problem we face is also an opportunity—for a learning experience and an opportunity for growth. Dealing with our problems, and realizing we can handle their weight, toughens us, enabling us to strengthen. With strength, we can then better deal with new problems as they arise in our lives.

> *"That which does not kill us, makes us stronger."*
> *—Friedrich Nietzsche, famous philosopher*

"Enough already!...No more opportunities for growth, please!"

> "If I were asked to give what I consider to be the single most important piece of advice, it would be this: Expect trouble as an inevitable part of life, and when it comes, hold your head high, look it squarely in the eye and say, "I will be bigger than you, you cannot defeat me."
> **—Ann Landers, Advice Columnist**

Stress is everywhere. For most of us it's in our home lives—even the world around us is enveloped with stress. We read the newspaper and it's full of things to be stressed about: wars, crime, and the latest disease or flu we might catch. Rumor has it that on occasion we can even find stress in our workplace. So, if you're feeling stress, you're not alone. Everyone is!

What is Stress?

Stress is a chemical change in our body that's created when our mind or body is under-strain. Stress is nature's way of telling us that something is not right, and we need to protect ourselves. The chemical change that stress creates causes changes in the way we think. It's tough to concentrate when we are under severe stress. We feel overwhelmed, anxious, scared, and often depressed. When we're stressed, we have too much on our mind at once making coping hard. Stress can make us angry and negative.

Change Causes Stress

One of the most common causes of stress is change. Even a happy change, such as a new baby or marriage, can cause a great deal of stress. We are always the least stressed when our life is just flowing. Change means there's something new to deal with, an unknown, and something we need to adjust to—and adjusting to anything creates stress. A new job, or even a change of jobs within a workplace, is very stressful. If you're new to your job and feeling stress and anxiety, it's normal. It will pass as you get to know people and become more familiar in the job.

Change leads to the unfamiliar, and that's scary. But without change, our lives stand still. Change is a great thing because it often leads to something better or happier. It is said that when a door closes, then another door opens. Think of change as exciting and an adventure—and then it will scare you less.

> *"What a caterpillar calls an end of their life, a butterfly calls a beginning. "* —Richard Bach

How Do You Avoid Stress?

Stress can't be avoided. Often people who try to **avoid stress** fully can even end up with **more stress**. You can't avoid stress, but what you can do is **reduce stress** and learn to live with it, so it doesn't affect your life nearly as much. In this section you'll learn techniques for dealing with your stress.

Let's look at some behaviors causing stress, which you should try to avoid:

1. Black and White (Extreme) Thinking

Black-and-white thinkers see everything in the extreme. For them, there is no middle ground. Every problem is earth shaking! Something is either totally right or a catastrophe. This causes stress because your workplace, and the world around you, rarely co-operate with your black-and-white thinking, seeing things exactly as you do. Black-and-white thinkers are very intense and stressed out. If you're this type of thinker, learn to relax. Practice adjusting to the idea that most things are neither black nor white. Every problem isn't a tragedy, but rather something less than you imagine. When you realize that you can handle most problems, your stress level will be reduced greatly.

"New Bulletin...It wasn't a terrorist attack at all. The city is in ruins because Sherry got a really big pimple!"

2. Negative Thinking

Negative thinkers see only what is negative or bad. If they won five million dollars in the lottery, all they would see is how much they would now have to pay in income tax. The glass is never half-full— it's always half-empty. Everything can be going great, yet a negative thinker will still find the one thing that's not perfect. Negative thinkers are always stressed out—because there's always something about which to feel miserable.

Negative thinkers are common in every workplace. Instead of focusing on what's good about their job, they always point at what they don't like. They do the same with coworkers, always finding fault in others. Negative thinking often goes back to upbringings, if nothing we did was ever good enough.

If you're a negative thinker, realize negative thinking causes you a lot of needless stress. Always finding fault and never being satisfied is tough on the brain. The solution is obvious: You need to change your style of thinking. Start to find things to be happy about instead of always looking at why you should be miserable. Whether a person sees the glass as being half empty or half full comes down to the attitude of the person looking at the glass.

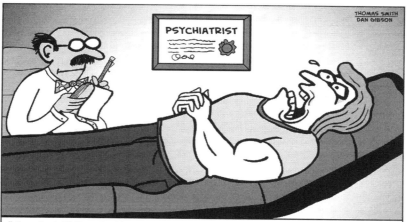

"So what if People Magazine named me the sexiest man on earth and I won the Noble Prize for Peace...I came second last in my 6th grade spelling bee, and I can't speak Chinese."

> "I guess I see the dark side of things. The Glass is always half-empty. And cracked. And I just cut my lip on it. And chipped a tooth." —Janeane Garofalo

3. Over Generalized Thinking

The Over-Generalized thinker is a person who decides if one thing is negative, then everything else has to be negative as well. Unfortunately, few things are ever perfect, so something is always bound to be negative and stress this thinker out.

"That proves it, everyone hates me."

4. Victim Thinking

Victim thinkers believe the world's always out to get them. It's as though they have been singled out for bad things to happen to them. They walk around with a cloud over their heads, always expecting an airplane or a meteor to fall out of the sky and knock them to the ground. They have been taught this victim thinking from the time they were children—often they have a parent who also thinks like a victim.

In and out of work, Victim Thinkers are always expecting the worst—they'll lose their job, they'll get sick, they're always waiting for the next disaster. They somehow believe that they've been singled out, and everyone and everything is out to get them. Of course, if you're constantly waiting for bad to happen, then you're always going to be anxious. The sad thing is that when you expect bad things to happen, negative thinking often leads to bad things actually taking place. If you're a Victim Thinker, then you need to learn to think more positive. Start focusing on the **good things** that can happen—instead of the bad.

"Tiger, I think you're a victim of identity theft. There are thousands of cats with the same name as you!"

4. Clairvoyant Thinking

A cousin to the Victim Thinker is the Clairvoyant. A Clairvoyant is someone who has psychic powers, who can see the future—and the future is always bad. Clairvoyant Thinkers believe everything they do will turn out badly anyways, so why even try! Why try to make friends, take on a project at work, or try anything at all? The outcome is always going to be the same—bad! Of course, this stresses this type of thinker out. The solution is to instead focus on expecting better things to happen. If we expect the worst, we'll likely get the worst. If we **expect better**, then we'll **get better.**

"Hello Mark, I'm cancelling our blind date...because I know you're not going to like me anyways."

3. Should Have Thinking

These thinkers rethink every decision they ever made, then moan about what they should have done differently. If they ordered the tuna sandwich, after it comes, they wish they'd ordered egg salad. If they did a particular job at work one way, they then think they should've done it a different way.

If you're this type of thinker you need to learn to accept, "What's done is done." Instead of using your energy stressing about a bad decision, look at ways to live with or fix choices that didn't turn out as you'd hoped.

"Darn, I should have given him my Master Card. I'm over my limit."

Don't Worry...Be Happy

Here's a little song I wrote, You might want to sing it note for note, **Don't Worry...Be Happy**. In every life we have some trouble, When you worry you make it double, **Don't Worry...Be Happy**.

—*Song by Bobbie McFerrin, from the Movie, Cocktail*

Life Tip

Everything in life falls into one of two categories—Either you can do something about it or you can't. If you can't do anything about it, what's the point in stressing out? **Try not to regret or stress about 'What you cannot change'.** It's a waste of energy and causes pain for no good reason.

Our Emotions

Our emotions are divided into two categories. Positive ones, such as love, excitement and joy. And ones to avoid—such as discomfort, fear, hurt, anger, guilt, inadequacy, embarrassment and loneliness. Everything we do, we do for one of two reasons, either to get **pleasurable emotions**, such as love or joy—or **avoiding negative emotions**, such as fear or being hurt. For most people, as much as we enjoy what's pleasurable, our stronger, or ruling emotions, are those emotions we're anxious to avoid.

Happiness and stress reduction happen when you appreciate all of your emotions. Realize that even negative emotions aren't the end of the world. Without taking risks, you reduce the good stuff in your life, such as new challenges and potential joys.

Overwhelm

There's an old expression, "The straw that broke the camel's back," which suggests a camel can hold just so many straws—and then one extra straw breaks the camel's back. In truth, the camel could probably hold a few more straws without a broken back, but the point is—there are limits. If an elevator has a capacity of 3,000 pounds, it doesn't mean 3,001 pounds will break its cord, plunging it to the bottom. But can it hold 10,000 pounds? So it is with us and being overwhelmed. **We all have our limits and breaking points.**

198

At times there's just too much to handle—too much work, or too many other problems. When that happens, the best solution is to break the work, or problems, into smaller pieces. Think of work, or problems, as being a large block of cheese. If it's too much to eat at once, then cut it in half. Still too much? Cut it in half again. Cut it until you have a manageable piece. What's the one task or problem you can handle right now? Or what's the one job stressing you the most? Why not tackle it first? Is there a task where you can ask for help, and lighten your load? Remember the old joke—How do you eat an elephant? *(One bite at a time!)*

How do you eat a giant peanut?…One bite at a time.

Depression

Did you know that over 25 million people in the United States and Canada suffer from serious depression each year? It's common. Depression, or any mental illness, is nothing to be ashamed or secretive about. If you suffer, **you must seek medical or counseling help**.

Letting Go of Blame: We use blame as a way of trying to control the rest of the world. Blame is an emotion which will eat away at you, causing you to feel angry and frustrated inside. It's nearly impossible to get along with someone when there is blame. *Try forgiveness instead*. Few things will free you from stress as much as 'forgiveness' will.

© 2003 Randy Glasbergen.
www.glasbergen.com

GLASBERGEN

"I learned about stress management from my kids.
Every night after work, I drink as much chocolate milk
as my stomach will hold, eat handfuls of sugary cereal
straight from the box, then run around the house
in my underwear squealing like a monkey."

Stress Tips and Techniques

We all experience stress, anxiety or coping problems now and then. Below are some techniques to try in stressful times. Some of these methods you can even try at work.

Stress Method 1: Deep Breathing

Deep breathing is nature's way of naturally relaxing you. When we breathe deeply we add additional oxygen to our blood, which relaxes us instantly. To deep breathe, begin by putting your hands on your stomach just below your navel. Breathe in very slowly through your nose, hold your breath for a few seconds, and then slowly breathe out through your nose or mouth. Repeat 5 times, or as many times as you need to feel relaxed.

Here is a deep breathing exercise that is wonderful for relaxation. It takes around 5 to 10 minutes to complete:

Begin by sitting in a comfortable place with your eyes closed. Take 5 deep slow breathes using the method above. Then focus on your feet, taking 5 or so slow and deep breaths, while making your feet feel totally relaxed. Then focus on your ankles, taking 5 or so slow deep breaths. From there move to focusing on your knees, then thighs, waist, stomach, chest, back, arms, hands and fingers, neck, mouth and chin, nose and ears, eyes, and finally forehead. Once you've done 5 deep and slow breaths for each body area, you should feel wonderfully relaxed!

Stress Method 2: Stretch

Muscles get tight when we are under stress, causing us to feel even more stressed. Take a few minutes to stretch. Stretch your back by arching it with your shoulders as far back as they will go. Then stretch your arms and legs out straight. Next, shake your hands and fingers. Finally, roll your head in circles, loosening your neck. You can even purchase a book of stretching exercises, or download stretching exercises from the Internet.

Stress Method 3: Straighten Up

When people are under stress, they tend to slump over with their shoulders and head down. Slumping restricts breathing and reduces the blood and oxygen flow to your brain. This makes your muscles tense and your mind tired. Straightening your spine, by sitting or standing straight, with your shoulders back, stomach in, and head high, will increase your oxygen flow and will relax your muscles, making you feel energized.

Stress Method 4: Exercise

Exercise has numerous benefits for stress release and as a method of coping during tough times. People who exercise also get sick less. The gym is not every-one's choice, so the key to exercise is find things you enjoy doing, whether that's walking (even in a mall), or hiking, swimming, or playing a sport. Exercise is important. When you're under stress at work, take a few minutes and do some exercises, such as deep knee bends or isometrics. Or go for a brisk walk during a break or at lunch. It'll not only reduce your stress, but energize you, as well.

Stress Method 5: Smile

Do we need something to smile about in order to smile? No, we don't. You can smile without any reason at all. Smiling loosens your facial muscles, making you feel better. That's why we enjoy smiling, because of how it makes us feel. So, when you're feeling down or stressed, smile for ten seconds, 5 to 10 times. If you need something to smile about, think of anything which makes you happy—a movie you saw, a pet, a child, or a happy memory. Happy thoughts will relieve your stress, too!

201

Stress Method 6: Fake It Until You Feel It

If you aren't in a great mood or feeling relaxed, you can be, by pretending. When you pretend to be in a great mood for one hour, by the end of that hour you'll feel better, guaranteed! So, pretend you're full of happiness and enthusiasm. Tell people, "I'm feeling great!" Laugh, whistle, sing—behave however a great mood feels like to you. Pretending works! And it will change how you feel.

Stress Method 7: Mood Changers

Here's my favorite 'mood changer' story. A few years ago my office was a mile away from an Indy-style Go-Kart track. My secretary was horribly depressed at the time. So, one day I said to her, "Let's take a break from work," and without telling her where we were going, I drove her to the Go-Kart track. Let me tell you, of all the people on the planet you wouldn't picture driving a Go-Kart, my 60-year-old secretary topped anyone's list. With the reluctance of a cow going to slaughter, I finally got her to sit in a Go-Kart, and nervously press the gas pedal. By the time she had done her fifth hot lap an hour later, I learned something, and so did she. It's impossible to feel depressed while driving a Go-Kart. Believe me! If Go-Karts were prescribed instead of Prozac, there'd be less depression today!

Find your own mood changers. At work that might be picking a song and singing it in your head—pick a happy song! Or doing a crossword or shopping at lunch. Away from work take time just for you, to do what you enjoy. This will lower your stress and improve your mood. Watch a movie or **dance!**

Stress Method 8: Giving of Yourself

When you're stressed, it's because you're focus is mostly on yourself—your situation and problems, what's bothering you! The best solution is to instead focus on helping someone else. It works because it's our nature to feel good about giving to others. Feeling good relieves our stress.

Think about ways in which you can contribute to others in the workplace. Is there someone else having a hard time you might be able to help, or even help each another? Or try volunteering. Giving to others gets you away from your own problems, resulting in feeling better about yourself.

The opposite, or the anecdote, for stress is: being at peace with oneself or contentment. And of course: **Happiness.**

So What is Happiness?

> "Happiness Depends on Ourselves. "
> —*Aristotle*

Aristotle lived in Ancient Greece. He is regarded as the father of philosophy—one of the greatest thinkers ever. Back when Aristotle lived, in 380 BC, around 2,400 years ago, there were very few books to read, and certainly no computers or television. Aristotle didn't have an iPod to listen to music, not even a radio. Energies back then went into just surviving, by gathering enough food to eat, burning whatever wood could be found to stay warm, and finding shelter. And, of course, fighting off dinosaurs—OK, there were no dinosaurs...there haven't been any for millions of years. But in Aristotle's day there were plenty of other dangers, such as wild animals and invading armies.

People had to get along just to help each other survive. Ancient Greece was one of the first civilizations in history where people formed cities. It was easier to survive and progress when they banded themselves together, than it was alone. In forming these cities, they had disagreements and problems, just like we do today. This is where philosophers like Aristotle came into the picture, to help people figure out how to get along.

Even today, the first order of business for people is still to survive. Someone who's fighting for survival, such as a person lost in a blizzard, doesn't ask whether they are enjoying life or not. Their goal is just to survive. In large part, that is why most people have jobs, to survive. Once we, as people, have the issue of survival well in hand, we then begin to ask for more from life than just merely surviving. Apart from surviving, we want **to be happy** too.

Even 2,400 years ago, people asked themselves an important question, a question people still ask each other today: "What is happiness and how can I be happy?" After all, isn't that the bottom line in life, **to be happy?**

So, what exactly is happiness then? And how does it apply to your job and to the workplace you are a part of?

The Secret of Happiness

People have been searching for the secret of happiness practically from the time there were people.

> ### *The funny thing is....*
> **The Secret for Happiness** really isn't a secret at all. The answer has been around as long as there have been people.

The problem is that most people confuse happiness with possessions, even though countless studies prove that millionaire lottery winners are no happier than the rest of us, and that people who end up paralyzed in wheelchairs from accidents, as a group, are no less happy than the rest of us. Buying something you really want, or taking a nice vacation can, of course, add to happiness, or at least lead to temporary happiness.

The problem is that most people tend to make their happiness conditional on things. There is always an **if** or a **but** involved.

We so often hear people say that they'd be happy in their relationship, if something were different. Or they'd be happy in their job, **but. . .** Or they'd be happy, for sure, if they had a new car. We make our happiness conditional on an army of things we have no control over, such as making more money, or other people behaving the way we want them to. Or even on some change in our life—or a possession we want. **If** we only made the change, or **If** we had that thing we really wanted, **then we'd be happy!**

© 1996 Randy Glasbergen.

"I finally figured out why cats spend so much time licking their paws—they taste GREAT! Try one!"

What is the Secret of Happiness then?

Aristotle sat and thought and thought about that question, because people 2,400 years ago wanted to know, too. He gave us the answer: ***Happiness Depends on Ourselves.***

Happiness boils down to one simple thing. It did 2,400 years ago, and it still does today: **Your Attitude.** You are the person who decides how happy you are going to be. So, if you choose to have a **Great Attitude** then you'll **be a lot happier**. If you choose to have a Rotten Attitude then you'll be a lot less happy. Happiness is not about, "Next year I'll be happy," or even "Next week I'll be happy." It's about making a decision right now to be happier. You don't need a reason. You can still have all the same problems. But problems or not, still **choose to be happier!**

People are happy in their jobs when they choose to be happy. Changing a job, without changing an attitude, rarely achieves anything, other than making you unhappy in your next job—then in the one after that. Choosing to have a great attitude at work will lead to being happy in your job. It will help you get more and succeed more—maybe not that day, but over time it will.

And one other thing...If you have a bad attitude at work, you'll take that same bad attitude home with you at the end of the workday. It will make you less happy in the other parts of your life as well. None of us has an **On/Off switch** for **happiness** or **unhappiness**. We take our moods with us everywhere.

"Don't forget to turn off the bad attitude switch before you go home to your family and friends."

I end this book with some of my favorite quotes on the subject of
Happiness and **How to be Happy**.

On Being Happy
HAPPINESS is not having what you want, but wanting what you have. —*Rabbi H. Schactel*
Be HAPPY while you're living, for you're a long time dead. —*Scottish proverb*
HAPPINESS is perfume---you can't pour it on somebody else without getting a few drops on yourself. —*James Van Der Zee*
HAPPINESS is when what you think, what you say, and what you do, are in harmony. —*Mahatma Gandhi*
Part of the HAPPINESS in life consists of not fighting battles, but in avoiding them. —*Normal Vincent Peale*
A man is HAPPY so long as he chooses to be HAPPY. —*Alexander Solzhenitsyn*
Whoever is HAPPY will make others HAPPY too. —*Anne Frank*
The biggest lie on the planet, is that when I get what I want I will be HAPPY. —*Source unknown*
When we recall the past, we usually find that it's the simplest things, not the great occasions—that in retrospect give us the greatest glow of HAPPINESS. —*Bob Hope*
HAPPINESS never decreases by being shared. —*Buddha*
Many people think that if they were only in some other place, or had some other job, they would be happy. Well that is doubtful. So get as much HAPPINESS out of what you are doing as you can. and don't put off being HAPPY until some future date. —*Dale Carnegie.*

Proof

Made in the USA
Charleston, SC
05 June 2013